The Promise of Nature

Ecology and Cosmic Purpose

John F. Haught

PAULIST PRESS
New York/Mahwah, N.J.

This book is printed on recycled ✪ *paper.*

Permission to use portions of the author's previously published work is gratefully extended: to the journal *Environmental Ethics* for portions of Chapter 1; to Orbis Press, *Liberating Life,* for some parts of Chapter 2; and to Georgetown University Press, *Minding the Time,* for substantial sections of Chapter 4.

Library of Congress Cataloging-in-Publication Data

Haught, John F.
    The promise of nature : ecology and cosmic purpose / John F. Haught.
        p.   cm.
    Includes bibliographical references.
    ISBN 0-8091-3396-2 (paper)
    1. Human ecology—Religious aspects—Christianity. 2. Nature—Religious aspects—Christianity. 3. Cosmology. I. Title.
    BT695.5.H38   1993
    261.8'362—dc20   92-41353
                                                                          CIP

Published by Paulist Press
997 Macarthur Boulevard
Mahwah, New Jersey 07430

Printed and bound in the
United States of America

Contents

to Evelyn

Introduction

In a recent speech Russell Train, who chairs the World Wildlife Fund, listed the main threats to our natural environment: the destruction of the rain forests, the erosion of our soil, the loss of sources of fresh water, the spread of deserts, the pollution of land, water and air, the alarming rate of extinction of species, global warming, and the thinning of the stratospheric ozone layer. Overarching all of these is the burgeoning human population: "Almost every significant threat to the environment," he says, "is contributed to and compounded by human numbers."[1]

It is disturbing to Train, who has been part of the environmental movement for over thirty years, that during much of this time organized religion has been almost totally unresponsive to the threats he enumerates. For that matter, so have other institutions like governments, big businesses and universities, but the obliviousness of religion to the environmental crisis, he notes,

> . . . has been nothing less than extraordinary. Here we have had one of the most fundamental concerns to agitate human society within living memory. Here we have issues that go to the heart of the human condition, to the quality of human life, even to humanity's

1

ultimate survival. Here we have problems that can be said to threaten the very integrity of Creation. And yet the churches and other institutions of organized religion have largely ignored the whole subject.[2]

Train acknowledges that here and there a few alert religious thinkers have dealt with the issues, but our religious institutions have been, he says, "largely silent and on the sidelines."

In response to the legitimate complaints of environmentalists like Train, I will be asking here whether the religions of the world, and in particular Christianity, have the resources to contribute anything of substance to the resolution of our current ecological predicament. I will be proposing in these chapters that they not only have much to offer, but that an adequate grounding of ecological concern requires the perspective of "eternity." The survival and flourishing of the earth is dependent on the survival and flourishing of religion.

Yet what Train says about religion's previous lack of interest in the state of nature seems to me to be accurate. The churches, synagogues, temples and mosques have not made much of a response to the ecological crisis until very recently. Nor have academic theologians. A few religious thinkers are now beginning to address the matter, but ecological theology still remains very much on the periphery of serious religious thought. In my own conversations with fellow theologians on the subject I am usually greeted with a sincere interest, but seldom with much sense of urgency. Having had the opportunity recently to review the resumes of a representative group of Christian ethicists, for example, I observed very little sustained concern for environmental issues.

As I seek an explanation for this lack of ardor I have to

admit that the thought has occasionally crossed my mind that perhaps Christianity and other religions, as they now exist, have in fact much less to contribute to an awakening of ecological concern than we might have hoped for. Do they perhaps inherently lack the resources to address what is, in fact, an unprecedented crisis? Are we now faced with a situation so novel, so beyond the realm of any religious mending, that it is foolish to expect significant help from our spiritual traditions?

And yet it also seems inappropriate for us to be too harsh in our criticism of religions for not having dealt very well with the ecological crisis. The environmental fate of an entire planet was simply not an issue during their emergence. It is too much for us to expect that they will provide us with ready-made answers to every new ethical emergency arising out of constantly changing historical conditions.

The ecological crisis, or at least our growing awareness of it, is unparalleled. And so the fact that religions are not ready for it need not in itself be a source of embarrassment. For that matter they have not been prepared to meet a lot of other historical events, such as the scientific revolution, the Enlightenment or the Holocaust. Today they are hardly ready for the fresh questions arising from new technologies, emancipation movements, the situation of religious plurality, the culture of postmodernity, the decline of communism and the emerging information age. Religions, since they are always bridled by the weakness of mortals, are never completely prepared for new events. After all, it is through their confronting unprecedented situations that they come to birth and receive their distinctive shapes in the first place. What is reprehensible, then, is not their lack of readiness to meet new crises, but their refusal to allow themselves to be transformed by them.

It is crisis that gives rise to religions and to major transformations of traditions. To Christians the most obvious example of dramatic metamorphosis precipitated by crisis is the refashioning of biblical faith that occurred in the wake of the catastrophe of Jesus' execution. This was certainly an event for which his followers could hardly be said to have been primed. Whatever sense they eventually made of their master's crucifixion did not leap out to them in bold face from the pages of the scriptures. The primitive Christian community had to struggle vehemently to wrest new significance from the traditional documents of their faith. Yet, out of the interruptive set of events associated with Jesus' death, they were eventually able to discover new life and to see things in an entirely fresh way.

It is conceivable also that the current ecological crisis, instead of leading only to complaints about the poverty of resources in our religious traditions, can become an opportunity and invitation to reinterpret their central themes in a radically new way. The present environmental predicament is an occasion neither for abandoning our religions nor for enshrining their silence on ecological issues. Rather, it could be a major historical stimulus to their revitalization. It is in the spirit of openness to the possibility of the creative transformation of religion that we here approach the question of theology and ecology.

In the following chapters, then, we shall be exploring the question whether religions, and particularly Christianity, have ecological significance. We shall occasionally touch on the wider world of human spirituality, but since planetary environmental abuse today stems predominantly from lands and cultures in which the Christian faith has been a strong cultural influence, we shall be narrowing our focus to a consideration primarily of the relationship between Christianity and the ecological crisis. Chris-

tianity has recently fallen under severe criticism for being
indifferent to nature's well-being, and so we shall be asking whether this chastisement is justified. If it is, then in
what direction must the tradition evolve if it is to be of
significance in the formation of an ecological ethic?

At the same time we shall be asking whether completely nonreligious, secularistic, or purely "naturalistic"
visions of the cosmos provide a suitable alternative to religious interpretations as a way of motivating us to care for
our natural environment. Since such a proposal has been
made by some ecologically sensitive scientists and philosophers, I shall begin, in chapter 1, with an examination of
the question whether a materialistic naturalism, and the
general mood of scientific skepticism that accompanies it,
are themselves capable of adequately innervating an ecological ethic.

We need to discuss scientific skepticism and its attendant naturalism at the very beginning, especially now that
scientists and theologians are mustering joint force against
the possible catastrophe that looms over the earth and its
living inhabitants. Skeptics and theologians are both seeking a solid foundation for ecological concern and action.
But if these two bodies are at bottom irreconcilable in their
ways of interpreting the universe, then the task of building consensus with respect to an ecological ethic may be a
difficult one to carry out. For that reason we shall undertake in the first two chapters a comparative evaluation of
naturalistic and religious ways of justifying moral concern
for the welfare of the earth.

I was fortunate to be present at a recent meeting of the
"Joint Appeal by Science and Religion on the Environment"
where I witnessed religious leaders and scientists, among
them a few prominent skeptics, issuing a consensus statement on the ecological crisis. The declaration proclaimed

that in spite of our differences we must all cooperate in attacking pollution, deforestation, global warming and the earth's other ailments. The statement is remarkable, not so much for what it prescribes, but for the fact that it indicates a struggle for moral unanimity among people with widely different philosophical and religious outlooks. Those who signed the statement range from fundamentalists to atheists, and yet they all agreed that the current crisis demands that we seek a common moral outlook.

What happened at this conference of scientists, theologians and religious leaders was only a beginning, though an important one. The opening sentences of the finally accepted document indicate the arrival of something new and wholesome: "We are people of faith and of science who, for centuries, often have traveled different roads. In a time of environmental crisis, we find these roads converging. As this meeting symbolizes, our two ancient, sometimes antagonistic, traditions now reach out to one another in a common endeavor to preserve the home we share."

There was none of the old animosity present at the two-day meeting. The sense of sharing that results from being grasped by a common cause stifled the fires of passion that might have arisen if the discussions had taken on their traditional pitch of intensity. The concern of the entire group was a pragmatic one, that of convincing elected officials, parishioners in rural and urban America, business leaders, scientists and engineers, and people everywhere, that the well-being of the earth is now in such jeopardy that all of us, no matter what our disagreements, must work together to put things right. In order to dramatize the seriousness of the message, the declaration emphasized that even people of faith and science can now see eye to eye on the urgency at least of this issue.

As it turns out, the majority of conference participants find no contradiction between science and religion. Many, in fact, are people who have spent much of their lives demonstrating the consonance of the two ways of interpreting the universe. Nevertheless, serious differences on the nature of reality still exist. To some participants in the conference the universe was created by God as a gift, whereas to others it is an absurd accident. For some the cosmos is imbued with purpose, but to others it is utterly meaningless. To some, the existence of life on earth is evidence of divine influence in evolution, while to others it is no more than a momentary cosmic fluctuation ultimately reducible to dead matter. In the face of such radical differences concerning the fundamental nature of the universe, then, I think we have to ask whether we will ever arrive at a true and lasting ecological consensus.

It is hard to imagine how any thorough transformation of the habits of humans will occur without a corporate human confidence in the ultimate worthwhileness of our moral endeavors. And without a deep trust in reality itself, ecological morality will, I am afraid, ultimately languish and die. Such trust, I shall argue, must be grounded in a conviction that the universe carries a meaning, or that it is the unfolding of a "promise." A commonly held sense that the cosmos is a significant process, that it unfolds something analogous to what we humans call "purpose," is, I think, an essential prerequisite of sustained global and intergenerational commitment to the earth's well-being.

Therefore, it is fitting that we begin our brief study by critically examining the ecological plausibility of those beliefs, myths or ideologies that extinguish any sense of nature's purpose. Doubts about cosmic purpose are abundant today, and they are nourished by some of our best scholars and universities. I will argue, however, that such myths provide a poor basis for ecology. Moreover, I think that in a way entirely consistent with science, nature may plausibly be interpreted as purposeful in the sense that it is a *promise*, a promise of ultimate meaning and beauty. And for this reason we may be persuaded to treasure it.

Because I hold this conviction, I was especially intrigued by the presentations of three prominent scientific skeptics present at the meeting to which I have referred. Carl Sagan, E. O. Wilson and Stephen Jay Gould, all of whom are famous for their renunciations of religious interpretations of the cosmos, each spoke on this occasion very favorably about religion's possible role in alleviating the ecological crisis. Long acquainted with their skeptical opinions, I was particularly attentive to their rationale for cozying up momentarily to the religious believers present.

Sagan is a renowned scientist and one of the main organizers of the appeal; Wilson is the founder of sociobiology, and Gould is a justifiably celebrated natural historian and author. All three are well-known for their agnosticism regarding religious ideas. They cannot accept the possibility that religions are telling the truth about reality. In other words, as far as they are concerned, religions are essentially illusory. Nevertheless, in spite of their doubt that religions can give us the truth about reality, all three agreed that religions can foster the kind of moral fervor that the environmental movement sorely needs. Each of them delivered essentially the same explanation for his fledgling affair with the religious community: while science can give us the facts about the cosmos, religion can provide us with the *moral inspiration* to act ethically in our dealings with it.

I think that this quite ingenuous proposal for joining religion to science in the enterprise of saving the earth needs to be examined more carefully. I can only applaud the genteel way in which these skeptics have set aside their philosophical convictions in order to find common ground with ideological adversaries. But I have to wonder whether it is completely honest for them to drink in this case so lustily from the stream of moral fervor that flows from what they have consistently taken to be the inappropriate and even false consciousness of religious believers. I am happy, of course, that they have done so. I think that in the matter of the planet's future, as on many other ethical issues, some degree of moral consensus may come about even when explicit justifications are in conflict. Yet the well-intended effort by the skeptics to co-opt the moral enthusiasm of the religions for the sake of ecology is especially puzzling, in view of the fact that it is only because believers take their religious symbols and ideas to be disclosive of the *truth* of reality that they are aroused to moral passion in the first place. If devotees thought that their religions were *not* representative of the way things *really* are, then the religions would be ethically impotent.

Thus, in the interest of deeper dialogue between scientists and theologians on the issue of ecology, I cannot ignore what seems to me to be the problematic nature of the justification Sagan, Wilson and Gould give for joining forces with the religious community. Therefore, in chapter 1 I shall take up the question of whether scientific skepticism provides an adequate basis for ecological ethics. Then chapter 2 will demonstrate how the theme of "cosmic homelessness," shared by members of both the religious and scientific communities, still underlies our negative environmental attitudes. Chapter 3 will discuss the view proposed by modern critics that the environmental crisis actually originates in religion. Chapter 4 will set forth what I consider to be the essential ingredients of a specifically Christian ecological theology. And chapter 5 will bring out the ecological significance of our establishing a strong sense of the connection between our personal destiny and that of the whole universe.

This book is in many ways an application to the issue of ecology of ideas I presented earlier in a work on science and religion, *The Cosmic Adventure*.[3] In the present work, as in the former, I continue to derive considerable help from some aspects of "process thought," even though I do not follow it slavishly, especially on the matters of divine creation and personal immortality. I should add that much of the following is adapted from material presented to various environmentally concerned organizations and academic groups over the past few years. I am grateful to all of them for the support they have given me as I have attempted to come to grips with the question of theology and ecology.

1

Ecology and Cosmic Purpose

Humans have always lived within the framework of myth. By "myth" I do not mean something untrue or opposed to "reality." Rather, I mean the set of stories, symbols and assumptions that determine our sense of what is real and what is important. Myths are the general visions of reality that mold our identities and give focus to our lives and actions. They have a profound impact on our conduct. Sometimes their influence is hard to trace, but it always lurks somewhere beneath the surface of our behavior. To understand why we act the way we do it is helpful to dig up the myths out of which our actions grow.

What are the myths, we might ask, that undergird the questionable human actions and policies that have placed us on the brink of ecological disaster? In raising this question we find ourselves before an extremely complicated issue. We are seeking to examine the broad outlooks that have promoted or tolerated environmental abuse. The chore is difficult, but circumstances oblige us to undertake it nonetheless. Even though the causes of the present crisis are manifold and complex, and not traceable simplistically to any single source, it is still essential that we try to say something about them.

At the roots of our culture I think we will be able to

find some general, and largely unexamined, mythic assumptions about the nature of reality that continue to nourish our toleration of ecological disintegration. Any serious grappling with contemporary threats to the welfare of nature demands, as we shall do shortly, that we look into the mythic themes that may be giving them sanction. I doubt that we can change our bad habits until we have examined and perhaps radically altered these motifs.

We cannot be indifferent, either, to the search for a "cosmology," a myth of the cosmos, or a broad vision of the universe, that *would* foster in us an appropriate respect for the nonhuman natural world. We cannot change ourselves by patchwork solutions or by psychological gimmicks. We are in need of a deep shift in cosmology. But is such a cosmology available today?

To gain acceptance today, we must confess at the outset that any ecologically positive myth about the cosmos must be scientifically credible. After all, it is from science that we would now gather most of the features of our cosmology. However, though it is necessary, science alone is an insufficient basis for an understanding of the universe. It is not clear that if nature possesses intrinsic value, purpose or promise, science could dig it out for us. By itself science cannot teach us exactly why our environment is to be treasured and preserved.

In fact, the more scientific our theories of the cosmos have become, the more questions have arisen about whether there is any inherent significance to the universe at all. For example, a renowned physicist, Stephen Weinberg, recently wrote that the more scientifically comprehensible the universe becomes, the more pointless it also seems.[1] Not every scientist agrees with Weinberg, but a recent book based on interviews with eminent astronomers indicates that a significant number still think of the universe as "pointless."[2] On the other hand, if we express our suspicion that the universe has a transcending purpose, or that it is stamped by the promise of some ultimate meaning, we seem to be soft-headed, unscientific and atavistically pious. Hence, most contemporary cosmology avoids the issue of cosmic purpose almost as though it were an infectious disease.

But I would like to press the question home as to whether we can go on ignoring or postponing indefinitely a consideration of the large mythic issue of cosmic purpose, or what philosophers call cosmic *teleology*, if we are truly interested in preserving our natural environment. If we care about the future of the earth, can we comfortably suppress all the troublesome questions that people have asked for ages about the character of the whole universe in which the earth resides?

Whether the universe is in any sense purposeful is, of course, an immense puzzle from which we are usually inclined to turn away because it seems that we are too small for it or that we are not in a position to solve it in any case. When the question of cosmic teleology comes up we feel uneasy, especially in intellectual circles. It is a topic for Gary Larson's cartoons about physicists in white coats writing complex equations, or for Woody Allen (who once said that he perceived intelligence in the universe except for certain parts of New Jersey). But it is apparently not a proper subject for those of us who abide in the world of common sense or who work in the academy. We may be willing to direct our energies toward improving the immediate terrestrial environment, but we generally see no connection between such pragmatic ecological activity and the question of an ultimate cosmic significance.

And yet, I would submit that it does make a considerable difference if we think about it seriously. If we believe that this earth is embedded in a meaningful rather than an ultimately pointless universe it cannot help but have a bearing on how we relate to it in our everyday lives. We cannot, without considerable impoverishment of environmental ethics, postpone indefinitely the question of cosmic purpose and its relation to ecology.

Does the new surge of caringness that many of us now feel toward our planet have the backing of the universe itself, or is our present preoccupation with ecological ethics merely the isolated outcry of a few lonely human subjects marooned on an island to which the rest of the universe is indifferent? Is the universe in its immense expanses of space and time largely unrelated to our moral passion, or is it conceivable that our local environmental concern is in some mysterious way the universe itself crying out for help? Do we inhabit an unconscious universe in which our ethical concern is only an accidental evolutionary anomaly, as the evolutionary biologist G. G. Simpson maintained?[3] Or is this concern itself the blossoming forth of a cosmic caringness that stems from deep down in the evolutionary process itself, as Thomas Berry holds?[4] Although such big questions cannot be answered by scientific investigation alone, they are not silly, and in fact they are of considerable relevance as we seek a realistic basis for ecological ethics.

Cosmic Pessimism

Many influential thinkers today are still convinced that the weight of science is clearly on the side of cosmic pessimism. In the introduction to this book I mentioned as examples the names of Carl Sagan, E. O. Wilson and Stephen Jay Gould. Such thinkers consider any vision of purpose in the universe to be archaic and illusory. They view all versions of cosmic teleology as no more than the psychological projection of our own human longings for significance onto a universe which as a whole is itself pointless. Any alternative to this view seems to them unscientific. Their aversion to teleology meets with the approval of many prominent pundits in the scientific, literary and philosophical communities. Indeed it is rare to find scientists, literati or philosophers publicly claiming that our universe has any point to it or that any transcendent purpose influences its evolution. But can this cosmic pessimism adequately nourish the vigorous environmental activism that many of these same thinkers, now hand in hand with members of the religious community, are calling for today?

The alternative to cosmic pessimism would have to be some version of what I shall call, with deliberate vagueness, the "religious" vision of reality. Yet to mention religion in conjunction with environmental ethics raises problems of its own. A great deal has recently been said and written about the part religion has apparently played in bringing about our ecological crisis. Although there is considerable exaggeration in this claim, there is also a certain amount of truth to it. The ecological legacy of religions is at best ambiguous. In a now famous essay Lynn White advanced the thesis, perhaps too often recited, that the origins of the present crisis lie in the Bible's giving to humans the status of "dominion" over the earth.[5] Although contemporary biblical scholarship would consider White's association of the Bible's notion of dominion with human arrogance to be quite naive, it is undeniable that western culture has often interpreted the idea as a sanction for subjecting nature to the human will, a license whose consequences did not become clear until the age of industry and technology. And Thomas Berry, himself a religious man, maintains that the Bible's looking toward a future messianic age has set loose a drive toward progress and limitless development that is draining the earth of its natural resources at a calamitous rate.[6] Once again, biblical scholars do not find the imperative to economic progress present in the pages of scripture, but the thesis is quite plausible that the Bible's millennial expectations have been ruthlessly contracted into policies promoting environmentally unsustainable economic growth.

Religion, many have complained, is the cause of, not the solution to, the ecological crisis. Critics have argued that the other-worldly focus of some major religions has led to our neglect of the natural world. Emphasis on the supernatural has made us ignore this world for the sake of the next. In biblically based cultures, an exaggerated apocalypticism (expectation of the imminent end of the world) has at times placed a sharp discontinuity between this miserably hopeless temporal world headed for doom, and the entirely new one that God will usher in on the last days. Viewed from this kind of religious perspective our present natural surroundings seem too provisional to merit the effort of conservation. If we fix our eyes only on eternity, as the saints and theology have urged us to do, then why should we hold onto the fleeting world of nature anyway?

There is no doubt that certain kinds of religious biases do sanction ecological disinterest. Our religious traditions need to undergo a thorough examination of conscience on this matter—something that they have only recently begun to do in a serious way. And in subsequent chapters I shall undertake a rigorous examination of the ecological value of religions. However, at this point in our brief study, instead of focusing on the possible religious origins of our environmental problems, it may prove illuminating first to explore some ecological implications of the antireligious posture that we are calling cosmic pessimism. Let us not immediately ask whether a wholesome environmental attitude can be promoted by religion, but whether an ecological ethic is congruent in any sense with the radically secularist conviction (whether implicit or explicit) according to which the final destiny of our physical universe is the void of meaninglessness? Our question, simply put, is this: can cosmic pessimism, which is the major alternative to religious cosmology, adequately support the ecological ethic to which many of its adherents are themselves committed?

By cosmic pessimism I mean the predominantly, but by no means wholly, modern view, now allegedly supported by science, that we live in a pointless universe, or in one that lacks any ultimate purpose. Cosmic pessimism is the conviction that the world has no transcendent origin and no divinely shaped destiny. It does allow that the world is partially goal-oriented or purposeful in some of its particulars, but it denies that the world is intelligible as a whole. The universe, the earth, life and human consciousness originate accidentally out of a process of unintelligible, random events worked over by an impersonal process known as natural selection.

While cosmic pessimism despairs of any final meaning to things, it does not see this metaphysical gloom as incompatible with a sincere personal and social delight in living. Moreover, the absence of objective purpose in the natural world gives us an ennobling status previously unacknowledged. For, since there was no meaning already present in the cosmos prior to our species' emergence, it is up to us humans to give meaning to things. We can thus rejoice in the unfettered absoluteness of our newly discovered creativity, previously obscured by religious myths. Spirituality had led us to believe that meaning was already resident in the cosmos, but now we see that our creative heroism can be the adequate ground of the world's meaning and of human happiness.

Materialist cosmic pessimism is the myth underlying numerous presentations of science today, and although it follows more from scientism than from science, it nonetheless makes its way into both academic and popular scientific treatises and textbooks. It does not always stick out in an obvious way, but it hovers over the works of many of our best scientific writers. Their disdain for cosmic teleology is manifested especially in their discussions of evolution which they consider to be absolutely opposed to any vision of cosmic purpose and, therefore, incompatible with religion.[7]

Gould, for example, complains that the reason Darwin's theory has not gained sufficient acceptance in our culture is that we are simply too unwilling (and uncourageous) to abandon the heartwarming religious notion that the universe has a purpose to it. In his view, seriously accepting Darwin's theory requires that we first give up any belief in cosmic teleology, that we surrender all hope that there is any sort of directionality to the universe, and that we embrace fully the view that lifeless matter alone is the ultimate ground of all forms of existence.[8] Similarly Wilson, although at odds with Gould in some respects, denies that there is any purpose to evolution other than that which is blindly determined by genetic history.[9] Many other contemporary scientific authors, too numerous to mention here, embrace the same creed.

The most widely read books on science today seldom entertain seriously the possibility of presenting cosmology in a way that permits the universe to be the embodiment of a purpose.[10] When religious people read this literature they are unfortunately (and I think unnecessarily) often forced to choose between "religion" and science. If science requires the abandonment of teleology, as cosmic pessimists insist, and religion requires that we embrace it, then logically speaking we would have to make an exclusivist choice: either science or religion. There is no room in between.

Interestingly, though, many of the same scientific skeptics who regard the cosmos as ultimately pointless and in the end reducible to mindless and lifeless matter, are quite passionate in their ethical commitment to ecological ideals. One might not expect them to be so disposed, but they obviously value the earth and the universe deeply and sincerely. Some of them, like Sagan, Wilson and Gould, are very persuasive, ethically speaking, about our need to protect the earth's biological diversity and integrity. Obviously they think earth's ecology is worthy of our care, and not just because it serves human purposes. To them it is valuable in itself.

However, without in any way casting a shadow on their sincerity, I hope it does not seem out of place to ask exactly *why* we should be so concerned about conserving any portion of a world which as a whole is finally empty of meaning and reducible to nothingness? Why should the same scientists who see no "point" in the whole cosmos, so vigorously oppose our reckless destruction of a tiny part of it? What I am asking here, to put it more directly, is whether there is sufficient substance in pure naturalism, that is, in an ideology devoid of any sense of the sacred, to inspire an ecological ethic. Or is it the case, as even some skeptics are now proposing, that we need religion to provide the moral passion for the ecological movement?

As I hinted in the introduction, their proposal that religion, though misguided in its beliefs, is still acceptable to the skeptics as a source of moral energy for the ecological movement, is at heart incoherent. I hesitate to call it dishonest since those who are advocating it have not really thought out fully the implications of their flirtation with the religious community. But if we look at the logic of the skeptics' inserting religion's moral energy into the ecological movement we cannot help noting some inconsistency. Let me try to spell out the incongruity of their proposed union as it appears to me.

To begin with, their reduction of religion to the status of being nothing more than a provider of morality fails to get at the heart of what religion is. Although religions are all associated with ethical conduct, morality is not necessarily their primary business. Moreover, people can be quite moral without being part of any religion. Our three scientific skeptics illustrate this fact through their exemplary commitment to ecological ethics. Many people simply do not need religion to tell them what is ethical and what is not.

Religion fits into our lives not so much as the source of moral imperatives, but as an answer to the question, "why be moral at all?" Religions respond to this larger question through their highly symbolic visions of the nature of reality. For example, biblical religion sees reality as the embodiment of an eternal promise of fidelity which we can expect to redeem even the most desperate situations. Those who believe in the truth of this vision, and who have internalized it seriously, will be aroused to moral activity, not simply because God says do this or avoid that, but in order to body forth in a human way the fidelity which undergirds all of reality. If divine promise and fidelity lie at the foundation of the real world, then our conduct must be congruent with the perceived nature of reality. We act morally not simply because of an external commandment, but because not to do so would be a deep act of violence against the nature of things. And so our moral actions seek to eliminate all that negates or cynically erodes human trust in the divine promise and fidelity.

The point here is that what grounds the morality is a fundamental vision about reality as such. The mythic conception of reality has primacy over moral aspiration, and provides its foundations. But, even more important (to stay with the biblical example), the necessary prerequisite of vigorous moral commitment to acts that express faithfulness, love and trust in our relations with others is the acceptance by faith that reality *as a matter of objective fact* is grounded in a divine promise of fidelity. Without a conviction that the religious vision is true, religious morality is inert. Without a belief that the vision bears a relationship to what is *really* the case, there can be no persistent ethical enthusiasm. If, for example, Christians began to doubt that a promising and faithful God really exists, this would render Christian morality baseless. A parallel case could be made for any of the other religions.

Our scientific skeptics, however, do not accept any religious vision as true. As cosmic pessimists, they see religions as bearing no relationship to reality at all. Nevertheless—and here is the irony—they still urge the ecological movement to take advantage of the moral fervor that comes from the religious communities captivated by the illusion that their visions are true. Scientific skeptics say that they are committed to truth, even to the point of endorsing an ethic of knowledge which makes it immoral to accept anything incapable of support by scientifically available "evidence." But in this case they are willing to allow the religious to remain mired in their illusions as long as these illusions inspire timely moral action. They are tolerant of spiritually intoxicated consciousness provided it is channelled in the right ethical direction.

Until this inconsistency is resolved, cooperation between religion and science on environmental matters will remain superficial. An ecological ethic remains impotent unless it is rooted in a commitment to the veracity of a shared vision of reality. We cannot get along simply believing "as if" the vision were true. Such dissimulation cannot kindle an ethical idealism. Accepting the moral effectiveness while jettisoning the vision that nourishes it smacks of duplicity. For this reason, the scientific skepticism represented by Sagan, Wilson and Gould is suspect as a foundation for ecological ethics.

Scientific Materialism

There are, however, even more cogent reasons for doubting the capacity of pure naturalism to fund the moral commitment we need to face the earth's present crisis. Earlier in this century Alfred North Whitehead undertook a reflection on the premises behind scientific skepticism and its companion, cosmic pessimism. He noted that they were usually rooted in what he called "scientific materialism." Recent developments in science, especially in physics, have challenged many of the ideas on which scientific materialism had been built. And yet, in spite of its being outdated, atomistic and mechanistic derivatives of this philosophical outlook still cling to scientific thinking. Whether it is Francis Crick's statement that all biology is ultimately reducible to chemistry and physics,[11] or French brain scientist Jean-Pierre Changeux's contention that all mental activity is completely specifiable by chemistry,[12] the meaning is clear: blind, lifeless and unintelligent matter, however mysteriously nuanced the concept of "matter" may be in contemporary physics, is alone the sole author and substance of all that is real.

Some version of scientific materialism, either "hard"

or "soft," still comprises the intellectual backbone of contemporary cosmic pessimism. What I am asking, then, is whether the "myth" of scientific materialism, either in its weak or strong forms, can provide the adequate philosophical basis for a fruitful environmental reverence. So many influential thinkers today still hold to some version of scientific materialism that it seems entirely appropriate for us to raise the question of its plausibility as the foundation of ecological ethics. Given the axiom with which we started these reflections, namely, that our general mythic outlooks will inevitably influence our particular actions, it is not a purely academic exercise that we are engaged in here.

Many scientists still think we can explain life and mind adequately in terms of chemical activity.[13] In spite of science's recent flirtation with more holistic models in various fields, the reductionist dream that we can fully specify the nature of life, and even of thought, in terms of their molecular makeup continues to animate laboratories and departments of science.

What I am questioning here, however, is not so much whether the reductionist ideal is logically or scientifically appropriate. I am convinced, for reasons that we cannot go into here, that it is not. Rather, at this point I am asking only whether materialism, which is the metaphysical underpinning of most scientific skepticism, is in harmony with ethical concern for the natural world. In response to this question I shall argue that scientific materialism and cosmic pessimism, though not necessarily opposed to a certain type of humanist ethic, are inherently at odds with a wholesome environmental outlook. Moreover, I think that we need a massive project of reeducation—at all levels, and especially in our universities—to expose the radically antiecological implications of the mythic worldview underlying most presentations of modern science. My own suspicion is that the spirited environmental concern of many scientific materialists today emerges only *in spite of* and not because of their underlying assumptions about the nature of the universe.

In a forceful declaration, the great American philosopher William James vented his conviction that scientific materialism could never serve the cause of conservation:

> That is the sting of it, that in the vast driftings of the cosmic weather, though many a jewelled shore appears, and many an enchanted cloud-bank floats away, long lingering ere it be dissolved—even as our world now lingers for our joy—yet when these transient products are gone, nothing, absolutely nothing remains, to represent those particular qualities, those elements of preciousness which they may have enshrined. Dead and gone are they, gone utterly from the very sphere and room of being. Without an echo; without a memory; without an influence on aught that may come after, to make it care for similar ideals. This utter final wreck and tragedy is of the essence of scientific materialism as at present understood.[14]

If this final wreck and absolute extinction is the last word about the universe, then why seek now to preserve it against the inevitable void that seems to be its destiny? James is asking, in effect, whether anything is worth saving if in the final analysis reality is devoid of the dimension that religion calls eternity. This is the question that leads our entire inquiry in these pages.

Yet many of the same pessimists who despair about the cosmos as a whole, and who think of it as ultimately reducible to lifeless and mindless "matter," are themselves passionately committed to the conservation of life and consciousness here on the earth. On the one hand they see no "point" to the universe, since only the void awaits the cosmic process; on the other hand they consider our earthly environment eminently worthy of our care and preservation.

To them there is no contradiction. The utter perishability of life, mind and culture that William James laments in his critique of scientific materialism does not really contradict our valuing and seeking to preserve these fragile things. In fact, the very indifference of the universe at large makes the local, earthly domain of life, by way of contrast, exceedingly precious and worthy of special preservation. Our awareness of life's precarious perch on the slopes of entropy requires that we regard it as much more than commonplace. Its very evanescence gives it an exceptional value when compared to the deadness of the inorganic background that comprises most of cosmic reality. According to the materialist myth, the improbability of life in this cosmic desert highlights its significance over against the triviality of a massively inorganic horizon. This precariousness alone is sufficient to arouse our instincts to save it. The very forlornness of life in the face of the universe's indifference sets it apart as special. We can build an adequate ecological ethic on the scaffolding of this harsh truth.

Thus, as it turns out, it may not be so remarkable after all that cosmic pessimists are numbered among the most enthusiastic proponents of environmental welfare. In their eyes any worrying about a wider cosmic purpose can distract us from the task of tending our earthly premises. Teleological speculations such as we find in the biblical hope for an ultimate perfection of creation, have no appeal. In fact, the conviction that there is a divine promise hidden in cosmic process might even take the urgency out of our present commitment to the earth as our true home.

The skeptic will ask: do not religions, especially eschatological faiths (faiths that hope in a future deliverance), allow us to postpone, or possibly abandon altogether, any serious concern for the immediate environment? Have not religions that proclaim an ultimate cosmic purpose allowed us to lapse into indifference about the present state of the earth's ecology? Does not the comfort of a meaningful final destiny allow us to tolerate too many abuses in the present? Is it not possible that the religious concern for transcendent heights lowers our esteem for the exquisite tissue of living forms that evolution has labored so long and hard, and against so many odds, to weave around this rock we live on?

The Ecological Inadequacy of Scientific Materialism

Cosmic pessimists prove to be formidable combatants. After attending to their bewitching proposals we might well wonder what ecological advantages could possibly reside in a religious interpretation of the cosmos. Can a teleologically inspired theology do a better job? At the very least we are challenged to rethink our theologies from the point of view of ecological concern. What sort of theological outlook could better support an environmental ethic? Would not cosmic pessimism with its acute sense of the perishability of life, consciousness and civilization be just as powerful as any religious eschatology in supporting our concerns?

I hesitate to think so. While its perishability may seem to be sufficient reason for cherishing life, a closer look will show that this is not so. A thing's perishability or fragility is not a satisfactory basis for valuing it. In fact, just the opposite is the case. Perishability depreciates value. The fact that things perish, including humans, makes us doubt their worth. The fact that we have to die puts our own sense of importance in question more radically perhaps than anything else. Thus, we typically deny our mortality and often strive to make ourselves somehow immortal within the span of our own lifetime.

Sheer perishability is a quality that detracts from anything's intrinsic worth. Therefore, actual reality must have some other attribute than impermanence in order to evoke our reverence. Scientific materialism, as far as I can see, cannot show what this additional element might be. It cannot adequately explain why life can be held to be intrinsically (and not just instrumentally) valuable.

Following a line of reasoning that I owe to Whitehead, I would argue that we value life not for its fragility, but for its beauty.[15] Beauty and fragility are not the same thing, even though they are companions. Beauty is the harmony of contrasting elements. Fragility is their tendency to fall apart. We spontaneously revere those things that unify a wide variety of complexity, nuance, or shades of diversity. But it is not the fact that these syntheses are prone to disintegration that leads us to esteem them. Rather, what arouses our appreciation is the symphonic patterning of differences into intense aesthetic unities when discord could easily rend them apart.

Living organisms or mammalian brains, for example, call forth from us a special valuation because they are integrations of an almost incalculable number and variety of components into intense unities of function and achievement. They have value, not because they are useful to us but because of their internal aesthetic harmony (or their potential for it). Likewise, what gives our earth's ecology its value, and at the same time explains its precariousness, is the fact that it is an instance of ordered novelty, of harmonized diversity, i. e., of beauty. Concrete instances of beauty are always in danger of decomposing into monotony on the one hand or chaos on the other. Instances of beauty, including the biosphere, indeed, do have an inherent instability that renders them temporary and precarious. But the precariousness is not itself the ground of their value. Rather their inherent beauty is their value. The goodness of things is rooted both in their internal beauty and, as I shall argue in chapters 4 and 5, in their contributions to a still wider beauty, not in the fact that they will eventually vanish.

Living things, like other instances of beauty, consist of an exquisite balance of order with novelty, harmony with complexity, and pattern with nuance. In such beautiful phenomena the novelty, complexity and nuance may threaten to overwhelm the order, harmony and pattern, and thus reduce them to chaos. It is because of the aesthetic tension between and among its contrasting elements that life systems have such appreciable delicacy. But their frangible quality is not the ground of the value we see in them. Precariousness is secondary to the synthesis of harmony and complexity that comprise the natural order.

Thus, our reverence for nature and its ecological patterning can be situated best within an aesthetic vision. Scientific materialism, on the other hand, separates beauty from the objective world, and this is the main reason that it fails as a basis for ecological ethics. It cannot acknowledge the intrinsic value of nature, for it takes beauty, and all values for that matter, as nothing more than human projections. The universe "out there" apart from human subjects is inherently valueless and purposeless. Value is the product of human minds alone, and therefore cannot be an objective aspect of the cosmos. Whatever value we see in the biosphere has its origins in our own valuing creativity rather than in an objective cosmic goodness existing independently of ourselves. To scientific materialism, as well as to the brands of humanism that are built upon it, nature as a totality is blind, mindless, neutral—in brief, valueless.

This widely accepted myth needs to be reexamined, today more than ever, because of its implied despair about the interior goodness of nature. To have an appropriate ecological ethic we seek a cosmological myth capable of recognizing objective value resident in the universe as it exists even prior to our projections. Unfortunately, very few of the governing forms of thought resident in our culture and in our universities today are capable of such recognition. In fact, the majority of them expressly deny that our valuations, because of their historical particularity and culturally conditioned character, can have any objective basis or reference whatsoever. Our valuations, even those we extend to the cosmos, are entirely determined by our cultural, linguistic and social conditioning.

Those who hold this opinion (and they are mainly academics) seem unaware of how easily it supports the exaggerated anthropocentrism that leads us to demean the non-human environment in comparison with which our own special, value-creative prowess shows up as so exceptional. Scientific materialists posit a fundamental alienation of the human mind from the impersonal, objective natural world out of which this mind is said to have accidentally evolved. The estranged mind is then able to take control of the universe to which it no longer belongs. Its sense of command allows it to subject nature to the mind's own intentions. A more radically anti-ecological myth is hard to imagine.

This point needs special emphasis. In spite of the fact that scientific materialism places life and consciousness on a continuum with the rest of nature, it splits the world apart once again. For it separates the allegedly creative human mind from the indifferent world of matter onto which we are said to project our culture and religion. It places a sharp discontinuity between the isolated human subject and the senseless universe investigated by science. This dualism in turn permits the kind of thinking expressed in the following remarks of a respected American philosopher (E. D. Klemke):

> From the standpoint of present evidence, evaluational components such as meaning or purpose are not to be found in the universe as objective aspects of it. . . . Rather, we "impose" such values upon the universe. . . . An objective meaning—that is, one which is inherent within the universe or dependent upon external agencies—would, frankly, leave me cold. It would not be mine. . . . I, for one, am glad that the universe has no meaning, for thereby is man all the more glorious. I willingly accept the fact that external meaning is non-existent, . . . for this leaves me free to forge my own meanings.[16]

Ecologists should shiver at such anthropocentrism. But Stephen Jay Gould, who is certainly far from being insensitive to the welfare of nature, expresses the exact same sentiments. After chastising us for rejecting the sense of cosmic purposelessness that he considers an essential implication of evolution, he reprimands us further for not seeing what a marvelous opportunity an objectively meaningless cosmos provides us for creating our own meanings. He thus echoes the sentiments of many modern thinkers: only in the experience of painting our own meanings on the face of a meaningless cosmos will we gain an authentic sense of our human significance.

Because of its inability to discover intrinsic value in the universe, this way of thinking has to be rejected as incompatible with any serious ecological ethic. If its advocates nonetheless support environmental causes this is not because of their materialist myth, but because of a residual moral and aesthetic sensitivity that is quite out of joint with their explicit philosophy. Their admirable ethical stance on the matter of ecology finds little support in their formal philosophical beliefs. If they consistently followed the materialist view that mind and life are completely and in principle reducible to dead matter, then, as Barry Commoner remarks, it would not be long before they would be proven correct. Any philosophy that theoretically resolves the animate realm into an inanimate one can hardly function as the foundation of ethical policies that strive to prevent this reduction from actually happening.[17]

A Theological Vision

On the other hand, if we look to religion or theology for an ecologically helpful alternative to cosmic pessimism we may be equally disappointed. For religions are often quite anthropocentric themselves. And when they are theocentric (God-centered) they are sometimes so focused on the supernatural order that they tend to discredit the natural. Is there anywhere a coherent theological vision that would not only tolerate but also positively promote a healthy ecological ethic? Is there a religious perspective on the cosmos that avoids excessive anthropocentrism and religious escapism on the one hand, and on the other provides a scientifically enlightened alternative to materialism and its offspring, cosmic pessimism.

In my own search for such a vision the closest I have come to it in the context of Christianity is the brand of theology that reinterprets the perennial religious vision of final purpose in terms of the cosmology of "process thought." Process theology, as this reinterpretation is called, uses concepts of the philosopher Alfred North Whitehead and his followers (especially Charles Hartshorne) who have provided an erudite alternative to scientific materialism as a way of understanding the cosmos and its significance. I cannot describe or defend this theology in detail here. In fact, I think that, like all theologies, it is still unfinished and in need of much development.[18] Nevertheless, it deserves special attention since it is the most systematic and scientifically enlightened attempt by recent theology to bring the cosmos back into a religious perspective. The search for an adequate theology of the environment cannot ignore the efforts of process theology. Without digging too deeply into it here I shall simply summarize two ways in which it might contribute to a theological vision of reality that would be more supportive of environmental concern than other forms of religious thought have been.[19]

Process theology is especially hospitable to the notion of evolution. Until theology takes evolution seriously it will not take ecology seriously either. Much of the reluctance of theology to engage the environmental issue in depth stems from its prior reluctance to think earnestly about evolution and its relation to God. Process theology, on the other hand, reconciles the ideas of God and evolution in a uniquely reasonable way. It understands God as the very source and stimulus of cosmic evolution. Instead of seeing evolution as an embarrassing scientific problem that theology can safely ignore, it views God as intimately involved in, though still remaining distinct from, the cosmic process. God is the creative *eros* that arouses the world to evolutionary movement, to life, consciousness and civilization. God is forever attracting the cosmos toward more complex levels of evolution. God is the source of the world's beauty and value, persuading the cosmos to body forth in its evolution ever more intense forms of ordered novelty.

This ultimate source of order is also the source of the novelty required for an evolving world. Not content with the status quo, God inspires a persistent restlessness in the cosmos. God is understood here as the source not only of order but also of the freshness and contrast that give beauty and therefore intrinsic value to all things. A theology that employs this conceptuality understands God as one who wills the maximization of aesthetic intensity in the cosmos. God's will is not only the creation of beauty but its increase as well. The divine dynamism promoting the intensification of beauty is the most significant "force" in the cosmos. It is the creative source of our emergent universe. God's will for us humans in this ecological cosmic vision is that we contribute our own lives to the adventure of enhancing the beauty of the universe. We are not the originators of value, but we may intensify its presence in the cosmos. Surely our ecological concern is a necessary contribution to this nurturing of cosmic beauty.

The evolutionary advance of the universe suggests a cosmic aim toward increasingly more intense forms of ordered novelty, that is, toward heightening the beauty and value of the universe. According to this theological cosmology the promise latent in our emergent universe consists of its adventurous aim toward beauty and the augmenting of experience that accompanies it. God does not compel the universe to evolve in this fashion, but acts only in a noncoercive, persuasive manner. The cosmos is not forced, but invited, to allow into itself continually more diverse forms of patterned novelty. It does not always accept this invitation in a straightforward fashion. It is allowed to wander and experiment with various forms of beauty. Our biosphere is one such experiment. It deserves our care, then, not because it is precarious, but because it is an instance of divinely inspired beauty.

In this theology humanity is not the only creative aspect of the cosmos. Our dignity is assured, but we are not the universe's only or essential reason for being. This universe obviously would not be same without us. Indeed, it would be considerably less intense in beauty and value. We need not follow the antihumanist kinds of ecology that see us simply as a cancerous growth on the cosmos. The universe, we can safely say, would be much impoverished without us, since for all we know humankind and its cultural creativity may be the most profound expression of cosmic beauty yet to have evolved. And yet our theology does allow that the biosphere would have objective value independently of our existence. The cosmos is not a value-neutral canvas that remains empty until we paint it over with our cultural creations. Nature, from start to finish, is itself a value-laden creative process.

In process theology the God of evolution allows for the play of chance in the emergence of species, for this God is not coercive power but persuasive love. A God of love does not force or compel, but allows at every level of cosmic evolution a certain indeterminacy which at the human level takes the form of what we call freedom. Each of us is called to contribute out of our freedom whatever we can to the intensification of cosmic beauty, an aesthetic achievement that includes society and culture but is not exhausted by them. Thus, process theology calls us not only to the preservation but also to the compounding of cosmic beauty. It goes without saying that such a vocation requires us to attend constantly to the welfare of all levels of cosmic reality without which this adventure of maximizing beauty would be impossible.

There is a second aspect of process theology that I would also like to highlight here. This is its conviction that what happens to our natural environment happens also to God. Unlike some traditional theologies that locate God "up there" totally apart from the world, process theology maintains that God's being, without in any way jeopardizing the divine transcendence, actually includes the world. God is not a reality that we reach only by leaving this world behind. Rather, God is the reality into which all events in the universe are finally synthesized and preserved as they aim toward a continually more expansive beauty. Thus we may say that the conservation and prolongation of nature's beauty actually contribute intensity and beauty to God's life. God is internally affected, indeed changed, by what happens in the cosmic process. When nature suffers, God suffers.

One of the reasons traditional religion and theology have remained "silent and on the sidelines" during the rise of the ecological movement is that believers in God have had a lurking and unspoken suspicion that, in spite of all the biblical instruction to the contrary, God really does not care all that much about the world. Therefore, why should we care? The "absolute" God of traditional theism often seems quite unrelated to the world, remote from its inner workings. In process theology, though, God is intimately related to the world. From an ecological point of view this means that when we work to save or intensify the beauty of the world we are thereby contributing aesthetic richness not only to our immediate, but to our ultimate environment as well. What happens to our world affects God. Hence, in this theological cosmology, it is not possible to be a worshipper of God without simultaneously loving and caring for our natural environment. Process theology provides us with a good theological reason to preserve the natural beauty of our world. In doing so we are instruments of the preservative care that is essential to God's actuality. Without our own acts of conservation we would not fully experience the caringness of God. For through our own conserving of nature we body forth the divine care for the world. Our own acts of adding to the diversity of nature are aspects of the cosmic process in which God lures the world toward more intense beauty.

Some theologians may be concerned that this notion of a God who actually feels the world, who is so intimately related to the temporality of the world, whose being includes rather than excludes the cosmos, jeopardizes the transcendence and perfection of God. In reply I must limit myself here simply to voicing my own conviction that though process theology still needs to undergo further clarifications, it has met these objections in a satisfactory way. Process theology does not deny that God radically transcends all things, or that God is absolute. Rather, it argues, in a manner consistent with the intuitions of religions, that God's capacity to feel what happens in the universe is relative to nothing, and is thereby absolute in that sense. God is the absolutely related one.[20] Nor does process theology deny that a God who changes is nevertheless still immutable in the only religiously meaningful sense of unchangeability: God is eternally faithful to the divine promise. Precisely by virtue of God's vulnerability and adaptability God manifests an *unchanging fidelity* to and care for the cosmos.

God is eternal, but God's eternity is inclusive of, rather than separate from, cosmic temporality. The notion of God's eternity can have religious meaning for us only if it also means that God weaves the world's evolutionary temporality into the fabric of the everlasting divine life, thus eternally preserving the value of those things that William James shows to be lost, according to the myth of scientific materialism. In Whitehead's own words God is a "tender care that nothing be lost."[21] Hence, God is the archetype, the supreme example, of the preservative care we are obliged to extend to our immediate environment. And we express our loyalty to this God by way of our own tender care of the biotic diversity to which we are linked, and the loss of which robs us also of our own being.

In terms of this theological cosmology the sin of ecological abuse is an aesthetic one, namely, that of settling for monotony and ugliness when it is possible to preserve and enhance the cosmic beauty that is nowhere more obvious than in the sphere of living beings. At root ecological neglect deprives not only ourselves but also God's inner life of deeper aesthetic intensity. It bears repeating: what happens to our environment happens also to God, our ultimate environment.

"True perfection," process thinkers say, "consists not in excluding everything but in including everything."[22] The classical idea of God, in spite of the best intentions of its adherents, tends to evoke images of God as excluding and even being unrelated to the world. Classical theism has persistently held that the doctrine of divine absoluteness means that God is not intrinsically related to the world. But this conceptualization of ultimate reality is not religiously satisfying.[23] Nor does it help us in our efforts toward an environmental theology. We best preserve the idea of divine transcendence not by making God unrelated to the world, but by envisaging God as *unsurpassably* related to it. Even though human sensibility and concrete religious experience are repulsed by the image of a relationless deity, the conceptual framework of classical theism promotes it nonetheless. And this distortion has evoked the often justifiable protest of ecologically concerned believers and nonbelievers.

For this reason ecological ethics needs an alternative not only to the myth of scientific materialism, but also to the classical theistic framework. I think that process theology is at least on the way toward constructing such a framework. Its theological vision of a divinely inspired cosmic adventure seems to me to provide at least the beginnings of a theological awakening to environmental concern. As I look at the theological alternatives I see none that comes closer to giving us a framework within which to pull together the insights of science and religion into a cosmology that encourages in us an evolutionary adventurousness as well as a preservative care that might inspire appropriate ethical attitudes toward nature. My hope is that this theology will, for earth's sake, continue to prosper.

2

Cosmic Homelessness

If a purely naturalist or materialist philosophy of nature cannot support an environmental ethic, neither is it immediately obvious that our religious traditions can do so either. As we indicated previously, several important scholars have even traced the origins of our environmental crisis to ways of thinking and acting associated with religion, and especially with biblical religion.[1]

The charge that religion in some way lies at the root of our reckless disregard of nature is a serious challenge to anyone who participates in any of the major religious traditions today. If it is merely an incidental or peripheral ingredient of religion that leads us to abuse our ecosystems, then we could in principle dispense with this component without throwing away the faith in its entirety. But if it turns out that the central and defining features of a religious outlook promote negative attitudes toward the natural world, then this might be reason enough for forsaking such a tradition altogether. If we considered our particular faith tradition essentially racist or sexist we would certainly have sufficient moral reason to abandon it. And so, likewise today we would be obliged to hand in our religious membership cards if our creeds turned out to be in some way *inextricably* connected with the human flight from nature or with any other negative attitude toward the cosmos.

What is it about religions in general that might lead us to question their ecological value? I shall argue here that, from the point of view of ecology, the single most problematic feature of the main religions is their dubious connection to the spirit of "cosmic homelessness." It seems that in many instances religions have fostered a sense that we do not really belong here in the cosmos or on the earth. This impression, stamped on human awareness by the theme of homeless exile present in the teachings of the major religions, leads many devout people to regard the natural environment as something from which to disassociate themselves in the name of religious integrity.

One of the central aspects of many religions is their teaching that authentic existence is "homeless," that pilgrimage, sojourning and rootlessness define our lives in this world. It is not entirely unexpected, then, that this feature of religious existence can give rise to a carelessness about our natural homeland. The origins of our ecological crisis may lie, in part at least, in a deeply entrenched suspicion by humans that the cosmos is not really our home. And the feeling of cosmic homelessness is, to a great extent at least, apparently "religious" in origin.

Whether religion actually requires that we experience the natural world as foreign territory far from our true home remains to be seen. But what seems incontestable is that, with some notable exceptions, the followers of religions have translated the indispensable ideal of spiritual homelessness into an ecologically objectionable *cosmic* homelessness. Nevertheless, this almost automatic association of religious with cosmic homelessness, I shall argue, is not necessary. It is possible to accept the sojourning, exilic character of religion without interpreting it as an imperative to remove ourselves from the natural world.

Cosmic Homelessness and Anthropocentrism

The root cause of ecological degradation is often said to be *anthropocentrism*. By placing an exaggerated emphasis on ourselves we rob nonhuman nature of its own intrinsic worth. This divestiture leaves us with the impression that nature is something useful only for our own designs. We perceive its value to be purely "instrumental" rather than intrinsic. And if nature is good only in the sense of being an assemblage of instruments to be wielded for human purposes, then it becomes vulnerable to our abuse as well.

But is anthropocentrism the deepest root of the problem? Is it not conceivable that our anthropocentric tendencies are themselves secondary symptoms of a more fundamental pathology, that of feeling that we are "lost in the cosmos"? I will suggest here that the anthropocentric exaggeration of our own importance is a reaction to the prior conviction that we are exiles here. To be an exile is to feel that one does not really belong, and this often means to be unaccepted by one's environment. When we feel that we do not really "belong" somewhere, we are most vulnerable to the feeling of shame. In ordinary experience we know how "home," except in dysfunctional situations, can function as a shelter from shame, and how not being at home may remove us from those powers that usually buoy our self-esteem. The loss of homeland is one of the most ignominious experiences human beings can have. Hence, if we habitually experience the natural world as a place of exile from our true home rather than as a source of sustenance and safety, we will inevitably hold ourselves aloof from it in some way, even while we remain bound to it. We will look elsewhere for our homeland and turn our attention away from the ground beneath our feet.

Anthropocentrism is one way of reacting to the feeling of not really belonging to the earth and the cosmos. It is our rebellion against the perceived foreignness of our situation. Abandoned in an alien country, we counter the stigma of shame by way of a groundless self-inflation, unduly exaggerating our own importance. If we can lift ourselves up above the natural order that seems to hold us captive, then, rather than seeing ourselves as belonging to the universe, we will begin to see the universe as belonging to us. It will seem to be beneath us, undeserving of our presence, and therefore not worth our tending. Its value will be measured only by what it can do for us.

Because it is a reaction to the more fundamental feeling of not belonging to the cosmos, a frontal assault on anthropocentricism will hardly be effective. We need, before that, to address the distressful feeling of cosmic exile to which anthropocentrism is a reaction. For, as long as we feel that we are not really at home in the natural world, or that we do not really belong to it, will we ever seriously care for it?

One might reply that nature has always treated us with harshness, or at least with indifference, and for that reason merits our distrust. Can we really feel at home in the face of this inhospitality? On the other hand, evolutionary theory instructs us that our species (as well as other forms of life) would probably not be here at all if the earth had been in every sense a *perfectly* congenial habitat for living beings. At least some degree of misfit with respect to the natural environment challenges life to evolve into new forms. The resistance of nature that humans often experience when they attempt to realize their own projects is, in the final analysis, part of the necessary set of constraints within which our own actuality is defined. But nature's harshness need not be interpreted as a pure hostility that warrants our repudiation of it. The fact that nature is often challenging to the point of severity is not incompatible with the fact that we still belong to it.

Unfortunately, not only religions but also modern secular thinkers have often made nature out to be our enemy. Bertrand Russell, for example, announced that the indifferent cosmos is really not worthy of us.[2] Likewise, Albert Camus interpreted the universe's insubordination to human desire as evidence of the final absurdity of reality.[3] And both Russell and Camus encouraged us to rebel against this universe in order to salvage our human dignity. Many scientific skeptics have agreed that the universe does not "care" for us. If so, one wonders why we should want to save its ecology for any other reason than that of perpetuating our own unexplainable existence?

We are coming to see, though, that the universe is not so unambiguously opposed to our being here as we used to think. Science is now making us more aware than ever of the pervasive cooperativeness of the manifold factors in nature that have somehow conspired to produce us. We are borne up by a comprehensive "caringness" that had previously eluded us. If in the long run evolution shows a disregard for individual organisms, and even for entire species, it is on the whole a process of far-reaching collaboration. For this we have every reason to be grateful rather than simply rebellious. Nature is home even if it is at times also a grim challenge. Inherent in nature is not only threat but promise.[4]

Religious Homelessness

I think we can take it as axiomatic that only those ways of thinking that allow us to look upon nature as a nurturing and sustaining "home" can be environmentally wholesome. But this canon immediately raises a serious question about the environmental worth of some of the world's religious traditions, including Christianity. For do they not teach us, especially through their mystical precepts, that we *should* feel dislocated from our natural environment? In promoting a spiritual homelessness religions have, perhaps unwittingly, instilled in their devotees an impression that they do not "really" belong to the cosmos. In that case the origins of our environmental crisis do seem to have a "religious" component.

There is no question that religions do idealize homelessness. The prophetic traditions, for example, go back to Abraham whose God called him to move from his ancestral home toward an unknown but promising future. And even though the theme of "the land" is prominent in Judaism, the period of wandering without a home is glorified by the prophets as the time when Israel could be closest to God. In the New Testament the Son of man, born in a stable, has "nowhere to lay his head" (Lk 9:58). Following Christ requires detachment from home and family (Lk 9:61–62). In much traditional Christian spirituality we are said to be only "pilgrims on earth." And how many Christian hymns have the theme that "this world is not our home"?

If we turn to the east, we observe that Hinduism sets forth as an exemplar of piety the *sannyasin*, one who becomes homeless for the sake of more intense union with the divine. And the Buddha's "Great Renunciation" required that he abandon wife, child and home. Examples could be multiplied. Clearly, according to the religions, homelessness is our most authentic state of being. Unless we become somewhat uncomfortable with "the world" or "this present age," we will hardly experience the incentive to break free from the shackles of immediacy. Only a continually "going beyond" present actuality brings liberation and fulfillment.

But for many religious people, in both the east and the west, the need to transcend "the world" in order to find salvation becomes a command to sever themselves from the cosmos. Religious homelessness seems to require the ecologically problematic feeling of cosmic homelessness. Religions, of course, promote homelessness not as an end in itself, but as a necessary moment in the quest for our true "home." But how often is this "true home" located in some setting quite divorced from the earth and the physical universe? And does not the location of our ultimate destiny beyond the cosmos inevitably render us careless about the natural world? Does not our cultivation of the ideal of religious homelessness lead us to tolerate an environmentally unacceptable attitude of cosmic homelessness?

The Bible is apparently not exempt from the charge that religion thrusts us out of our natural homeland. Biblical religion is distinctive in making the events of human history, rather than aspects of nature, the primary points of encounter with God's redemptive action. Salvation history prohibits any easy return to a purely natural existence. The prophets implacably rebuke those who seek healing by returning to the fertility rites of mother nature. They point us toward the coming of God's salvation at some future time in history. For the present, hope and trust are sufficient to heal us. The purely natural order is not solace enough. We need something wider and deeper which only the future can bring us. And we cannot grasp it with our rituals and sacraments alone. We need the "word" of God's promise.

Biblical religion does not completely uproot pagan celebrations of the earth's goodness. Rather, it colors the archaic ceremonies over with historic meanings commemorating the acts of God in history. Israelite religion historicizes the world to such an extent that there is really no independent concept of nature. "Nature" as understood by Greek philosophers or modern scientists is foreign to Hebraic thought. Is not this fact itself sufficient reason for our suspecting the ecological value of biblical faith? Does not its relentless pursuit of future historical salvation, its constant reference to a divine promise, divert us from appropriate devotion to the physical universe?

Today there is much understandable idealizing, especially by religiously sensitive ecologists, of the piety of "pagans" and native peoples who lived (and live) closer to nature than we do. While the complete restoration of prescientific piety is neither possible nor desirable today, there is a sense in which its "sacramental" spirit, such as we find in primal religions, is considered essential for the shaping of a contemporary ecological theology. We shall examine this prospect in more detail in the following chapter. For now, though, we need only observe that biblical religion seems to some ecologically concerned theologians to have a shadow side that has crushed the life out of those pagan forms of religion that approach nature with ardent reverence. By idealizing Abraham the Bible seems to have encouraged in us a feeling of restless wandering that perhaps prohibits an ecologically satisfactory relation with the earth.

But does this historical and personal restlessness require the abandonment of a sense that the earth is still our home? Does the prescribed religious journey inevitably require that we render ourselves "lost in the cosmos" to the point of despising the natural order as an intolerable shackle on our wandering spirit? If so, then we would have to conclude that our revered spiritual teachings foster the very posture that provokes, as a defensive reaction, an environmentally calamitous anthropocentrism.[5]

And yet, those of us who embrace the teachings of religious traditions need not and, I will contend, should not simply abandon the disturbingly exciting ideas about the fundamental homelessness of our being. To do so would be a violation of some of the most sacred, and ultimately fulfilling, features of the traditions we have inherited. It is, of course, imperative that we prune from these traditions all that is exclusivist and oppressive. But their precepts about learning to live with a spirit of pilgrimage, of being on a long journey, of being detached from "home," cannot be ignored. Ecological theology cannot be purchased at the price of this precious imperative.

Fortunately, as we shall see, the confusion of religious with cosmic homelessness is avoidable after all. We can, at least in principle, preserve the lofty ideal of religious homelessness without requiring the environmentally unhealthy conviction that we do not belong to the universe. Developments in both theology and science make this union possible today. We may even find a way to interpret religious homelessness in a manner that leaves us firmly embedded *within* the natural world. I shall follow up on this proposal later in the present chapter, but before doing so I would like to review some influential interpretations of both science and religion that continue to champion the escape from nature that we are calling cosmic homelessness.

Scientism and Materialism

Our sense of being exiled from nature originates in myths and other forms of thought, according to which we humans are only accidentally present to, but essentially absent from, the cosmos. The roots of this attitude go back to ancient forms of religious dualism. However, in modern times, it is not just religion but also the dominant assumptions of our scientific culture that have encouraged our estrangement from the natural world. Scientism and its offshoot, scientific materialism, have given unprecedented intellectual support to the belief that we do not really belong to the cosmos.

For example, scientism (according to which only the methods of science can yield true knowledge of reality) puritanically segregates the human knower from nature. By isolating the knowing subject from the object-world, scientism repudiates the ecological vision according to which all entities in the cosmos are somehow interrelated and interdependent. In scientism the knowing subject is no longer considered to be a part of the scientifically known universe. In order to be appropriately disinterested, and therefore "objective" about the world, the scientific subject is set apart from nature. And even though in other respects science tells us that humans are part of the cosmos, that we are materially continuous with it, a scientistic epistemology excuses us, cognitionally speaking, from the universe. As Michael Polanyi has observed, scientism constructs a picture of the universe in which we ourselves are absent.[6]

What we referred to in the previous chapter as "scientific materialism" also contributes to the modern sense of cosmic exile. This philosophy reduces all reality to lifeless matter. It is based on assumptions going back to the now problematic physics of the seventeenth century, and we need look only briefly at these assumptions to see how they support the sense of cosmic homelessness that still pervades our ecologically insensitive forms of modern thought.

Chief among them is the belief that "primary qualities" (such as mass, momentum, shape and position) are the most concrete aspects of nature. Unlike secondary qualities (color, taste, sound, smell, texture) which require the presence of a perceiving subject, primary qualities are allegedly "out there" in the world in a permanent sort of way. They are said to have an "objective" character independent of any participation by an observer. While secondary qualities seem to require our own creativity, primary qualities are held to be objectively "real." This distinction of primary from secondary qualities initially seems quite harmless. But, if we adhere to it too strictly, it eventually leads us also to locate ethical values and religious symbols within the same insubstantial arena as that occupied by secondary qualities. Value, beauty, importance and purpose will seem, therefore, to depend for their reality also on our own existence and creativity. (Thus, they are sometimes called "tertiary" qualities.)

Such an assumption obviously robs nature of any importance it might have apart from us. It allows nature at most only an "instrumental" significance. That is, it bestows on nature no other value than that of being important for our own projects. It may not seem so at first sight, but such a perspective on things severely exiles us from the cosmos. It gives primacy of being to the colorless, valueless and humanly uninteresting aspects of nature, while beauty and value proceed from the insubstantial realm of human creative caprice. In this cosmological setup there is a seemingly unbridgeable gulf between the perceiving and valuing human subject "in here" and the "real," material, and valueless world of primary qualities "out there." This means nothing less than that we are cosmically homeless, strangers to the cold indifference of the allegedly "objective" natural world of primary qualities.

Those who adopt the assumptions of scientific materialism sometimes allow that we may usefully entertain the *illusion* that we have overcome this exile. Through the psychological mechanism of "projection" we are permitted to paint over the neutrality of nature with our own imaginative, artistic, poetic and religious inventions. These fictions may momentarily give us the impression that the universe is hospitable. However, if we follow with logical rigor the canons of materialism we are eventually compelled to acknowledge that underneath all our projections lie only the inherently valueless and meaningless "primary" qualities uncovered by classical physics. And if these are the fundamental constituents of the "real" world then we shall forever remain exiles from it. We will still be "lost in the cosmos."

Since they do not allow for any vital interrelationship of the human subject with nature, scientism and materialism cannot support a truly ecological vision. As we noted earlier, the proponents of scientism and materialism are themselves often vigorous supporters of environmental causes. But their explicit doctrines about nature, if they are thought out consistently, can only lead to an attitude of cosmic homelessness. In the final analysis a thoroughgoing scientism and materialism would logically justify our disregard for an environment that seemingly fails to nurture our estranged subjectivity. There is little hope for our recovering the feeling of truly belonging to the cosmos as long as our culture and universities continue to harbor (as they indeed still do) these by now worn-out assumptions. Until we completely revise our contemporary scientific cosmologies we will not be able to shake the persistent suspicion that the "real" world is radically different from our projections. And so we shall continue to harbor the conviction that we are without a home in the valueless universe lurking beneath our perceptions and human constructs.

But can we improve on this modern view of a valueless universe, one that makes us seem, in our search for meaning, to be so out of place? Recently a number of notable and worthy cosmological alternatives have come forth, although departments of science and philosophy are still suspicious of many of them. Earlier in this century, for example, Alfred North Whitehead convincingly demonstrated that the primary qualities taken as fundamental by materialism are really not so "primary" after all. Rather they are themselves mathematical abstractions that have been logically mistaken for concrete reality.[7] Moreover, recent developments in science have toppled the assumptions of classical physics that gave such gratuitous solidity to the primary qualities. Both relativity and quantum physics, for example, have shown us that the scientific observer is no longer an exile from, but an integral participant in, the universe. And contrary to the cosmic pessimism based on classical mechanics, recent astrophysics indicates how hospitable the material universe has always been to our eventual arrival here. The initial conditions and fundamental physical constants that determine the structure of the universe are remarkably suited to the emergence of life.

If we compare recent scientific ideas to the mechanistic schemes of the nineteenth and much of the twentieth century, we are compelled to acknowledge that they add up to a remarkable breakthrough in cosmology, and one with considerable environmental implications. Even physics, the science that formerly seemed to exile us forever from nature, now concludes that the existence of life and mind is not so surprising after all, given the specific nature of atoms and stars from which we evolved. Matter, it turns out, has not given birth to living and thinking beings as grudgingly as we used to conjecture. Apparently the universe at large is not indifferent to our being here.

However, in spite of such developments in science, much of our intellectual culture today continues to cling to

the classical assumptions on which scientism and materialism are based. Philosophy, psychology and even literary
criticism commonly suspect that the symbols and myths
that might reconcile us to the earth, have only a derivative,
projective or humanly "constructed" character. Symbolic
expression, whether of poetry, art or religion, seems to be
as ontologically thin as Galileo's and Locke's secondary
qualities.

For example, novelist and critic Walker Percy writes
that it is precisely our ability to signify through symbols
that shows us to be strangers in the cosmos. ". . . man,"
he said, ". . . is the only alien creature, as far as we know,
in the entire Cosmos. . . ."[8] In Percy's theory of semantics
our capacity to point by way of signifiers to referents beyond those signifiers (and I assume these would include
the symbols of religion as well) implies that our symbolizing selves must somehow exist *outside* of the cosmos. He
holds that a very important dimension of our being (the
symbolizing self) occupies a totally different kind of terrain from that of nature.

Percy doubts that we would have the freedom to signify one thing by way of another unless the signifying self
stands freely beyond the natural environment. His rather
"gnostic" way of explaining, and also justifying, our cosmic homelessness is very alluring. Like most dualistic
views it has a tidiness about it that appeals to the puritani-
cal mind-set of modern scientism and literary criticism, as
well as to much traditional spirituality. But I think it is
fundamentally mistaken, based as it is on a scientific
worldview that is now passing away. And if its "disin-
carnate" character were thought out seriously and consistently, it would eventually prove to be environmentally
noxious as well.

Why could we not learn instead to look at our symbolic activity in a more cosmological fashion? At the same time that (psychologically speaking) it is certainly our own creative production, our symbolizing is also the work of a more primordial "creativity," that of the universe in which we are ourselves rooted. Since we, too, are part of the universe our humanly symbolic activity is, in a very literal sense, a self-disclosure of the cosmos rather than something that originates outside of that cosmos. Our symbolic life is *the cosmos itself* seeking adventurously, through us, to expand and intensify its own being. Our symbols do not require, as a condition of their referential capacity, any alienation of ourselves from the universe. More fundamentally, our "subjective" symbols are expressions *of* the universe (subjective genitive). And our religious symbols are the means through which the cosmos itself gropes toward its future.

As long as we think of our signifying activity as though it were the activity of strangers stranded in, but still somehow outside, the universe our symbols will not deeply take hold of us. Most important, however, they will fail to connect us sympathetically to the cosmos. For we will still suspect that they are nothing more than our own fickle projections. And when we do so, we shall no longer be able to be grasped by them in any profound way. If we think of our religious myths, for example, as nothing more than soothing human inventions they will hardly be able to provide the motivation for an ecological ethic.

As an alternative to the modern suspicion that such symbols reveal only our own desires, I would propose that we begin to think of our myths, metaphors and religions not simply as psychic creations (which in some sense they are, proximately speaking), but more fundamentally as the flowering forth of the universe itself. Cosmologically speaking, these symbolic "constructions" are the universe's, and not just our own, response to the mystery that calls it and us into being. We need to outgrow our long-held premonition that humanly symbolic creativity is groundless, ethereal gesturing of lonely subjects adrift on the surface of an uncaring planet. But we will not be able to envisage our symbolic creativity in a cosmological way until we have become convinced (as I suspect most of us still are not) that we *ourselves* are, in a very literal sense, a natural germination arising from the depths of the universe, and not aliens who have strayed here from some other world.

Theology and Cosmic Homelessness

However, it is not just scientism and materialism that have taught us to accept on intellectual grounds a posture of cosmic homelessness. For modern theology as well has been pervasively influenced by some of the same assumptions that in other quarters have led to scientism and materialism.

Perhaps the most obvious instance of theology's flirtation with cosmic homelessness lies in existentialist forms of religious thought. Rudolf Bultmann, for example, turned to the philosophy of existentialism in order to rescue Christian faith from an outdated cosmology. Christian faith, he declared, is really about freedom, not nature. Thus, by directing the focus of theology away from the determinisms of nature and toward the inward realm of existential subjectivity, he and his students established a very influential way of thinking about faith that provides much of value for hermeneutical theory, but few resources for the development of an ecological theology.[9]

Furthermore, Bultmann's existentialist theology uncritically embraces the materialist-mechanistic conception of nature whose negative environmental consequences we have already underlined. By separating the realm of freedom sharply from the determinisms of nature, existentialism makes human subjectivity inherently alien to cosmic reality. Given the classical mechanistic notion that nature is rigorously determined, we can appreciate existentialism's vigorous attempt to salvage human freedom. In this respect, it has made valuable contributions, and we need not be excessive in our criticisms of it. But in order to rescue our freedom from the "world-machine" of classical mechanics, existentialism often requires a separate realm for this freedom, a domain clearly outside of nature. Thus it, too, exiles the core of our existence from the cosmos. Obviously a theology based on this dualism of nature and human existence cannot take the natural world seriously enough to ground a sturdy environmental ethic. Theologies that employ existentialist concepts, worthy as they are in other respects, are likely to perpetuate the sense of cosmic homelessness and the restrictive anthropocentrism that it inevitably evokes.

Such also seems to be the case, at times at least, even in the otherwise ecologically wholesome theology of Karl Rahner. Rahner helpfully emphasizes that human existence is "spirit in the world" (*Geist im Welt*), and his Christology situates the Christian mystery firmly within an evolutionary universe.[10] But in one of his later essays he gives theological legitimacy to the feeling of being "lost in the cosmos." Like existentialist thinkers (including Martin Heidegger) he interprets the essential feeling of "forlornness" in a way that seems to alienate us from the natural order. Science, he observes, has given us a fresh awareness of our smallness and apparent insignificance in the universe. But instead of allowing this insight of science to embed us even more firmly in the fabric of the cosmos,

Rahner follows the kind of thinking we find in cosmic pessimists who dwell on the incongruity of humans finding themselves in the cosmos at all. Awareness of the utter contingency of our existence in this immense universe, according to Rahner, can elevate us "above" the cosmos:

> Today, and more than ever in the future, human beings and Christians are also going to have to realize more clearly and more radically that their very *recognition* and *acceptance* of the fact of being lost in the cosmos actually raises them above it. . . .[11]

And, in still more disturbing language, he adds:

> If people have to give up their feeling of being at home in the universe in exchange for a feeling of not being at home, *which reflects the character of their religious experience*, then this is at root a *legitimate* element of humankind's fate.[12]

I would suggest that our current environmental crisis requires that we subject to criticism any such theological language because it carelessly identifies religious with cosmic homelessness. We must seek new ways of affirming our spiritual homelessness without turning it into an endorsement of cosmic homelessness.

In still other, and more subtle, ways contemporary theology persists in segregating human existence from the natural world. It does so especially where it has come under the spell of psychology and the social sciences.[13] These disciplines themselves still often share the assumptions of materialism with its attendant cosmic homelessness. They tend to interpret religious symbolism (like other aspects of culture) as something done *on* the earth by our species, rather than as something the earth does through us. They view our symbolic expression as imaginative "world-building," or "world-construction," superimposed upon rather than flowing out of, the natural realm. Accordingly, religion is now seen, even by some theologians, as just one more vaporous product of human creativity.

A number of contemporary theologians, in fact, now envisage religion and theology simply as human construction. Probably the most obvious example can be found in the work of Harvard theologian, Gordon Kaufmann.[14] Even though Kaufmann was earlier quite critical of existentialist theology's dualism of mind and nature,[15] his recent theological publications are built on the thesis that religious and theological ideas are nothing more than *human* constructs. He offers a very Kantian picture of religion and theology according to which the "noumenal" reality of God can in no way be represented or come to expression in our religious symbols or theological concepts. Therefore, revelation is an obsolete theological notion. Religions and theologies must be accepted simply as our own *human* imaginings or constructs.

It cannot be denied that some very helpful insights into religion may be gained by viewing it from the point of view of its relative, historically conditioned and socially constructed character. But an unfortunate reductionism occurs when our dizzying new awareness of the "constructed" character of religion becomes the dominant or exclusive way of looking at so thick a phenomenon. Such reductionism does seem to characterize Kaufmann's work. The cosmological assumptions underlying his theological program are not clearly distinct from those of scientism and materialism. His rigorously Kantian segregation of an unavailable noumenal world from the available phenomenal one has not yet escaped the seventeenth and eigh-

teenth centuries' questionable divorcing of primary qualities from the "phenomenal," and allegedly fictitious,
realm of secondary and tertiary qualities. In both cases
imaginative and creative human subjects are pictured as
estranged from the "real" world, a world which they can
approach only by covering it over with a perceptive or
imaginative clothing of their own making, and which may
have little or no relation to the underlying substratum itself. In Kaufmann's case religion and other forms of symbolic expression do not emanate from or reflect any ultimately "real" world, but are instead only exercises of the
human imagination bounced off of, rather than expressive
of, the noumenal realm. The symbols and ideas of religion
are thus located ontologically in the same sphere as secondary (or tertiary) qualities. And so, the origin of religious
meaning is ascribed primarily to the human subject, since
the "objective" world apparently lacks, or is reluctant to
disclose, any possible inherent value or meaning.[16]

This kind of theology still suffers from the lack of an
ecological spirit. It ignores the underlying continuity of
humans with the cosmos. If it were taken with complete
consistency, it, too, would fail to ground an adequate environmental outlook. A theology shaped by ecological wisdom, on the other hand, would nest us and our religious
symbolism more intimately within nature. It would propose that our religious world-construction is, more fundamentally speaking, a natural emergent from an already
value-permeated universe which is home to us as well as
our religions. Instead, however, much contemporary theology is still shaped by the dualistic, and therefore cosmically homeless, way of thinking that we have just observed in the case of Kaufmann. It makes humans out to
be primarily value-creating or meaning-projecting beings,
and it sees the physical universe as little more than the

stage upon which the creative and constructive human religious drama plays itself out. The cosmos, in this view, lacks the intrinsic value or meaning that might nurture our religiousness. It is left up to us isolated subjects to provide whatever significance the cosmos appears to have.

Certainly, as modern thought has helped us to realize, creativity is one of our main human attributes. But the human sciences and the theologies based on them at times insinuate that there is no meaningful creativity going on in the universe outside of ourselves. Early in the modern age Cartesian dualism separated cognitional subjectivity from the cosmos, locating it in us humans alone. Whitehead has corrected this dualism through his "reformed subjectivist principle" which attributes subjectivity to every actual entity in the universe.[17] In the past century, however, the temptation has been to wrest *creativity* from nature by placing it in us humans alone. This expulsion of creativity from nature contributes, no less than the earlier exorcism from nature of all experiential subjectivity, to a devaluation of the entire nonhuman cosmos. It blinds us to the possibility that creativity is a quality inherent in all entities.

The central anthropological image governing this modern approach is that of *homo faber* (literally "man-as-maker"). A one-sided pursuit of this image leads to the conviction that authentic human existence is attained only in those moments when we are creating. The capitalist work ethic, Marxism and existentialism all contribute to the enshrinement of this icon. They pronounce "unauthentic" any ideas or attitudes that obscure awareness of our purely human productivity. The natural environment then appears as little more than material waiting to be turned into *homo faber's* concoctions. If human subjectivity is authentic only in moments of grasping its own creativity, then nature will typically be seen as barren stuff whose value is only subservient to our creative will. Obsession with the *homo faber* image leads us to suppress the fact that our constructive potential is itself the outcome of a multilayered cosmos whose own emergent creativity has given birth to us long before we expropriated this creativity as our own exclusive franchise.

To the extent that Christian theology has come under the spell of existentialism, Marxism, the humanistic social sciences, and more recently post-structuralist criticism, worthy as these may be as sources for theological correlation it, too, is vulnerable to the excesses pertaining to the *homo faber* image. Theology also at times gets carried away with the theme of human creativity and ignores the more foundational cosmic resourcefulness in which we are rooted. It implicitly sanctions an excessive humanism and a corresponding devaluation of nonhuman nature. In doing so it continues to support the sense of cosmic homelessness that underlies our environmental crisis.

Religious Homelessness and Ecology

Now, to return to our main question: can we feel at home in nature while at the same time remaining faithful to the religious need to be continually restless until we rest in God? Can we accept the worthy ideal of religious homelessness without bringing along with it a feeling that we are lost in the cosmos? Or will the universe and the earth continue to be little more than the point of departure of our religious pilgrimages? Will the nonhuman natural world, then, continue to be the victim rather than the beneficiary of our religious sojourning?

For religions, "home," in the fullest sense ultimately means nothing less than the incomprehensible "mystery" surrounding our lives and inviting us to enter ever more deeply into it. Religions require that our lives not become embedded too comfortably in any domain short of this ultimate goal and horizon of our existence. Fidelity to our traditions demands that we accept religious homelessness as an aspect of genuine journeying toward home. But it would be ethically intolerable to interpret religious homelessness in a way that allows it to sanction an environmentally unhealthy cosmic homelessness. So our question, once again, is this: precisely how are we to connect a feeling of fully belonging to nature with the ideal of religious pilgrimage? How are we to prevent our religious journeying from becoming a flight out of the cosmos? This, I think, is one of the most important questions facing the religious traditions today as they seek to come to grips with the ecological crisis. Until we settle this issue we will not be able to persuade people that religions do have something to contribute.

Fortunately, science can itself come to our aid as we seek to address the matter. For scientific cosmology now instructs us that *the universe itself is a restless adventure,* one that coincides with and supports, rather than always resisting the spiritual self-transcendence enjoined by our traditions. It is our good fortune to live at a time when the cosmos, thanks to the advance of scientific knowledge, appears more and more like a grand epic story within which our religious journeying is itself an episode, not an extrinsic intrusion. Instead of being a whole new book with no connection to previous chapters of the cosmic narrative, our religious searching can be interpreted as an extension of the cosmic adventure itself.

As we now know from science, nature has always been creatively restless. Science itself has come to represent the cosmos as a story, or perhaps even better, as an adventure. Adventure, according to Whitehead's definition, is the aim toward novel forms of order, or toward increasingly wider beauty.[18] Viewed over the long haul, the universe appears to be this kind of adventure.

Thus, in a certain sense, we can now envisage the entire cosmos, and not just religion, as a pilgrimage, as a long story of "homeless" wandering. The cosmos is not a static point of departure for the religious journey; it is itself a journeying. The religious adventure may now be situated within a more comprehensive cosmic peregrination. The context and precondition for humanity's spiritual adventure is the universe's own inherent "instability." The cosmos, therefore, is a fellow traveler, not something we merely pass through and then leave behind on our sacred voyage into mystery. Ultimate mystery seeks out the total universe and its history, not just restless human souls. Nature is a companion to human spirituality, not a temptation to inertia. It appears as a constraint or prison only when our concepts of it abstract from the processive, creative, intersubjective and exploratory character of all physical reality. In religion's long search, nature's evolutionary experiment reaches toward its own fulfillment. All of creation, as St. Paul says (Rom 8:22) longs for fulfillment. Many modern religious thinkers (especially Teilhard de Chardin) have been aware of this for some time, but we are only now beginning to appreciate fully its ecological implications.

The most expressive metaphor for what science finds in nature today is no longer law, but story.[19] There have always been narrative undercurrents in some aspects of scientific theory, but since the time of Darwin science has become increasingly dramatic in its representations of what goes on in the natural world. Now our entire cosmos seems to have unfolded gradually in a fifteen-billion-year

+ Hubble helped Einstein - story
Fr. Lemetre gave him the
right math.

Cosmic Homelessness 63

chronicle of adventurous wandering. Astronomer Fred Hoyle rightly calls it the most fascinating story ever told.

Physicist Brian Swimme observes that at its most basic level, the universe is not so much matter or energy or information, but story.[20] And, like Thomas Berry, he proposes that this cosmic story is deep and extensive enough to embrace the story (or stories) of religion. The encompassing cosmic story may also now serve as a common narrative strand around which to weave the results of our interreligious and intercultural encounters.[21]

Science did not take on this narrative countenance without a struggle. Swimme recalls the familiar anecdote according to which Albert Einstein himself turned away from the narrative implications of his own research. Einstein's mathematics indicated that the universe had a singular origin and that it then unfolded in a gradual manner. But the famous physicist doctored his equations so that they would fit more closely his predilection for a law-bound cosmos. And it was only after Edwin Hubble convinced him that the red-shift phenomenon shows our universe to be expanding that Einstein admitted he had blundered.[22] Nowadays it is common scientific knowledge that the galaxies, stars and planets have themselves evolved out of simpler configurations. They have come into being as part of an unimaginably lengthy and complex cosmic story.

Swimme observes also that story

> . . . forced its way still further into physics when in recent decades scientists discovered that even the fundamental interactions of the universe evolved into their present form. The laws that govern the physical universe today, and that were thought to be immuta-

Long periods of time when nothing happens.

ble are themselves the results of developments over time. We had assumed that the laws were fixed, absolute, eternal. Now we discover that even the laws tell their own story of the universe. That is, the Cosmic Story, rather than being simply governed by fixed underlying laws, draws these laws into its drama.[23]

I have suggested with Whitehead that we may even more aptly characterize the cosmic process as an adventure story.[24] The cosmos is itself a risk-taking, a struggle from simplicity toward more intensely ordered novelty and complexity. Like any adventure it is precarious because its groping toward further complexity is not always rewarded. There are many regressive moments, episodes of chaos, and simply flat periods of endless waiting. In any grand narrative, though, there are going to be long spells of time in which nothing much happens. But the backsliding and the stretches of tedium are clearly not the whole story. Viewed over the long term, adventurous developments have occurred, such as the emergence of life, mind and human culture. And the birth of religion may be the most adventurous development of the cosmos so far.

Why did our species became so religious? Cosmologically speaking, it was not in order to escape the earth, or to construct imaginative schemes that would provide a fictitious sense of nature's hospitality. Rather, religion came about to sustain and prolong the adventure that was already going on in the universe. Religion arose out of an inherently adventurous universe whose struggle toward novelty it now seeks to keep alive and extend further. The restlessness that propelled the cosmos on its fifteen-billion-year pilgrimage has not yet died out. At the present phase of evolution it continues to stir within the hearts of

Religions as The extension of The Cosmic adventure — our construct speak of a deep reality — Through Vaguely

those who realize their destiny lies in surrendering themselves and their world to mystery.

Summary and Conclusion

The "long search" of religion is an extension of the cosmic struggle toward "perfection" (a term Whitehead employs to designate the widest possible harmony of contrasts, or beauty).[25] Thinking of religions as a prolongation of the cosmic adventure may prevent our disconnecting their summons to a life of homelessness from the cosmos, which itself has always also been far away from "home." The theme of homelessness is so integral to our religious traditions that we cannot simply ignore it. Instead we may learn to appropriate it in a scientifically intelligent and an environmentally healthy way. Religious people uninformed by the findings of science can too easily interpret nature as though it were a restraint. They often experience our natural habitat as though it were holding us back from the spiritual journey. But now science itself teaches us that the universe is itself an adventurous journeying. Religious searching is not opposed to, but instead expressive of, the adventurous nature of the universe itself. We need not, therefore, make our earthly environment a victim of religious homelessness. We and the earth and the universe, all together, still live in "exile" from our universal destiny, but not inevitably from one another. Thus we are not obliged to feel "lost in the cosmos" in order to embrace the homelessness that religion requires. This should make a difference in our evaluation of the ecological significance of our religious traditions.

We are Spirit in earth —

3

Religious and Ecological Integrity

Imagine that all human beings were suddenly removed from the face of the earth; that our cities, highways, forests and fields were stripped of all human presence. What would be the implications for ecology? Within a few years vines, weeds and trees would begin to spread out over the crumbling pavements. Buildings would begin to fade and disintegrate. Many species of animals that had never previously inhabited urban settings would wander in from the countryside and invade the city streets. Birds and beasts would find friendly quarters in the crevices of metal and concrete structures. Within several hundred years, the traces of our civilizations would already be partially obscured. Streams would have cleared up, and though some lakes and lands would remain permanently impaired, pollution, deforestation, desertification, etc., would have undergone a dramatic reversal. The departure from the earth of its most pernicious predator would have permitted the survival of endangered species on land and in the air, oceans and streams.

Clearly, then, it is not so much a crisis of nature but a crisis of culture and civilization that we are dealing with here. We do not grasp the true nature of the earth's ecological distress if we focus only on what is happening in nature. We have to look at the cultural factors that shape our social, economic and political life. For it is out of the ways that humans have organized their lives together that the crisis in nature arises.

The experience of painful symptoms is a signal to look for the underlying causes. When we have personal physical and psychological discomfort we look beneath the symptoms to the deeper reasons for the disease. Likewise the present travail of nature invites us to look beneath the nauseating pollution and mindless destruction of life for the hidden origins of the earth's illness.

Recently a great deal of scholarly energy has been devoted to the symptomatology of the environmental crisis. Much of this research has concluded that the proximate origins of the crisis consist, for the most part, of the economic immoderation that is rapidly using up our nonrenewable natural resources.[1] In all parts of the planet today, for instance, agricultural practices are eroding fertile topsoil, which in some cases requires many thousands of years to produce as little as one inch. The search for new farm land leads in turn to deforestation, desertification and even climatological transformations (for example, in the case of the burning of rainforests) which most scientists now agree will rapidly damage the entire ecology of the earth. Likewise, industries everywhere are polluting the air, water and soil, causing the spread of disease, birth defects and other maladies, many of which we are only now becoming aware of. The quest for energy sources to meet rising industrial demand depletes the earth's reservoirs of fossil fuels, scars the land with strip mines and persuades some nations to resort to the use of dubious and dangerous forms of energy. Meanwhile, fishing and hunting practices are leading to the extinction of species that took millions of years for evolution to create. And the

[handwritten note:] The IMF agreement with So Korea requires S. Korea To construct (bey) 6 Billion Nuclear Eng. Plant 3)

massive mobilization of military machinery, designed to protect our economic structures and shore up our "way of life," provides, both in its testing and actual implementation in warfare, some of the most violent and permanent environmental destruction in the world today.

To a great extent the industrial, agricultural and military habits that are ruining the biosphere are supported by styles of economic thinking nurtured by our universities and think tanks. In current economic theory, for example, there is the assumption that any economic system must expand indefinitely if it is to provide sustenance for large numbers of people. The gross national product must keep on growing or else the economy will stagnate. This way of thinking influences candidates for political office and leaders of nations who, oblivious to ecological consequences, declare that "economic growth" must continue.

Clearly there can be no solution to the predicament we are in without a reform of economic activity and thinking. But can such radical reform in the way we organize our lives together ever take place without a sea change in the deeper and more remote mythic and spiritual dimensions of our existence? Today an increasing number of ecologically concerned authors doubt it.[2] Many of them are now emphasizing the need for a wholesome religious vision as the basis for our maintaining the integrity of nature. But what would a healthy or "integral" religious vision look like? And precisely how could it promote the wholeness of our ecosystems? These are questions that need more penetrating responses than they have received so far.

If the health of the environment depends in some way upon the integrity of our religions, then we must spell out precisely what criteria a religion must meet in order to function in a manner that will motivate us to take care of the nonhuman natural world. In this chapter I shall be

setting forth what I consider to be the minimal require-
ments for an ecologically wholesome religious life. In doing so I shall be looking in a very broad way at the religious dimension of human life and then show how our
failure to sustain religion's own integrity will inevitably
prove to be injurious to the environment.

I have been assuming throughout this book that most
readers are aware, to some degree at least, that we are
faced today with an enormous ecological crisis, and that, if
unchecked, it will lead eventually to planetary catastrophe. It is not my task to spell out concretely what we each
need to do in order to save our earth. Books and expert
opinions detailing the concrete steps needed to preserve
the environment are abundant. Instead my main concern
here is to seek any possible resources in our religious traditions that might nourish our efforts to avert the impending
calamity. Can religions provide something more basic than
a cheerleading function for the environmental movement,
which to a large extent seems to have originated and been
carried on independently of explicit religious motivation?

The Ecological Ambiguity of Religion

The prospects for such a contribution by religion, we
have already noted, are not clearly established. The relationship of traditional religions to the status of the earth's
ecology is, at best, ambiguous. We cannot always be certain that religions do care all that much about the natural
world. Some of them are very other-worldly in their focus.
Some Christian fundamentalists, for example, look forward to the final passing away of this world in an apocalyptic conflagration. For some kinds of religion, even the complete destruction of the natural order does not come as bad
news. To environmentalists, therefore, religions can be

"bad news" precisely because they are, to their followers, such good news.[3]

In 1973 a Catholic archbishop spoke of the "anti-human" character of "worship of the environment" derisively calling it "the new cult of nature unspoiled." He thought it would be better if we continue to view nature as our enemy lest the wilderness overtake us and mastodons once again roam the ruins of Chicago.[4] His views are still shared, to some degree at least, by many Christians and even some Christian theologians. Many of them still look upon this earth as nothing more than a "vale of soul-making" whose purpose is to provide a place of trial and purification for the human spirit. In this vision care for nature is not very important. A few theologians and religious leaders, though now decreasing in number, fear that the environmental movement will distract us from the human issues of justice and peace.[5] And still others think of environmental activism as a purely secular interest with no relation to religious existence.

Because of religion's association with cosmic homelessness, a number of ecologists have been highly critical of its traditional expressions. In their disillusionment some of them have turned to one or another brand of naturalism as a more promising alternative. They have enshrined nature itself as the sole creator of all, fully deserving of our human worship. According to some so-called "deep ecologists," humans are only an insignificant evolutionary development that has turned out to be a menace to the natural world out of which it emerged. Accordingly, the sooner we humans disappear from the scene the better off the earth's life systems will be.

I think we have to admit that the question of religion's value for the ecological movement is still up for debate. It is not sufficient, as I argued in chapter 1, simply to cite the potential significance of religion's moral fervor. Unless religious visions tell us something about the actual shape of reality, such that its visions would lead us spontaneously to embrace an ecological ethic, then they are virtually useless for our purposes. However, I continue to maintain that religion is much more than just a reserve of ethical energy that can now be channeled into ecological action. Over and above its moral potential I believe (contrary to Sagan, Wilson and Gould) that religion can, in fact, tell us something ecologically important about the real world.

The reversion to a naturalism devoid of any sense of the eternal will not, in the final analysis, help solve the ecological crisis. In fact, as we shall see shortly, naturalism is a dubious and somewhat parasitical outcome of the disintegration of religion in modern times. Religion itself is not the cause of the crisis. Instead I shall advance the thesis here that the ecological crisis is to a great extent a consequence of the *disintegration* of religion. Hence, it is in the best interests of the earth's ecology not to seek the demise of religion, as secularism argues, but rather its conservation. Along with the call to preserve the earth's biodiversity, we are summoned to heed the voices that are pleading today for the preservation of the richness and diversity of the world's religious traditions. The cause of ecology is dependent on our maintaining the integrity of religion.

We can hardly deny that in shaping peoples' attitudes and ethics religious visions of the universe still play one of the most dominant roles in all aspects of human culture. So we cannot but inquire whether religious understandings of reality have any great stake in salvaging our natural environment. If they do, then on what basis and in what way might the point be upheld?

Theology has not yet convincingly demonstrated how

The job has not yet been done.

religion might be conceived of as *inextricably* connected with ecological concern. It is, of course, possible to find in religious teachings many specific items that might reinforce an environmental ethic. For example, their emphasis on humility, the avoidance of greed, the ideal of simplicity, the exhortation to tread lightly upon the earth, the goal of universal compassion, the spirit of sacrifice and detachment—all of these would seem to make religion a very positive contributor to our reconciliation with nature. Furthermore, one can cite numerous passages from sacred writings, or point to certain religious motifs (such as the Jewish Sabbath or the Indian notion of nonviolence, *ahimsa*) as evidence of religion's potential for augmenting the status of life on our planet. And, of course, there are special saints like Francis of Assisi and explicit environmental declarations from religious officialdom, such as the papacy, The World Council of Churches or the American Catholic bishops.

It is a great sign of religion's ecological promise that such statements are now forthcoming. And yet, in my opinion, none of these instances of concern for nature has established with sufficient firmness the inescapable link we are seeking between religion (including Christianity) and ecological ethics. I do not wish to belittle the environmental importance of those elements of religion that I have just listed, but purely secularistic thinkers have issued the essential ingredients of an environmental ethic even without any explicit need to refer to the sacred, to God or some transcendent dimension as religions do. And the ecological movement has produced many secular saints who rival Francis of Assisi as exemplars of sensitivity to nature.

So if we are going to make the case for religion's ecological indispensability today we have to dig deeper. We need to do more than simply invoke occasional passages of scripture such as the psalms that glorify nature. We

RELIGION = "CONSCIOUS ORIENTATION **" to MYSTERY"

cannot be content simply to recite Jesus' lyrics about the lilies of the field, or devote ourselves to Taoist and Buddhist precepts. We have to inquire whether there might not be some much more basic and pervasive way in which religion can be understood as supporting ecological integrity. I will argue here that religion does have such a fundamental and irreplaceable role to play in sanctioning the environmental movement. However, in order to make this point, I must first identify those features that I consider essential to religion.

Religion — *as SPIRITUALITY*

Since I shall be dealing with Christianity more explicitly in the following chapter, here I shall be speaking in a very general way of what makes for an ecologically wholesome religion. Broadly speaking, I understand religion as a conscious orientation by human beings toward an incomprehensible, gracious and saving mystery which in our cultural context we usually call "God," but which others may call by different names. Muslims call it *Allah*, Hindus *Brahman*, Buddhists *nirvana* or *dharma*, Lakota Indians *wakan*, Taoists the *Tao*, etc. For some, this mystery has a personal face, while for others "personality" does not adequately symbolize what they take as ultimate. John Hick thinks that all the religions provide ways by which people may experience a transformation that orients their lives to correspond with an ultimate "Reality."[6] John Bowker observes that religions have in common the trait of steering us through the most intransigent limits on life that all of us encounter.[7] My own preference here is to think of religions generally as ways of orienting us toward the inexhaustible, enlivening and liberating depth of reality that we may call by the name "mystery."

Like Einstein & This Course Spirituality 101 COM until 48

Sagan REASON Intelligence The Mind

The various designations of this mystery found in the many religions cannot all be reduced to some common essence. We must avoid the temptation of thinking that all religions are saying the same thing. Nevertheless, they do seem to share, at least for the most part, the impression that every sacred name points toward something infinitely more fulfilling, truthful and real than can be expressed by the name itself. This horizon of ultimate reality or truth is what I mean by "mystery." We may understand religion, then, as our orientation toward this domain of mystery.

When it is wholesome this movement toward mystery has four distinct aspects: sacramental, mystical, silent and active. To say that religion is "sacramental" means that it employs concrete symbols derived from our ordinary experience (and especially from nature) in order to talk about the extraordinary world of sacred mystery. When I say that religion is "mystical" I mean quite simply that it attempts to give us a sense of an "other" than ordinary dimension of reality, of a "oneness" or unity that embraces but also transcends or lies somehow "beyond" the empirically available natural world. In saying that religion has an aspect of "silence" I mean that genuinely religious people eventually realize how difficult it is to speak accurately about divine mystery, and so they are at times tempted to say nothing at all, to seal their lips in silence and to quiet their imaginings about the ultimate reality in which they are enfolded. And, finally, to say that religion has an "active" component means that religion is concerned in some way with changing or transforming the world. We shall describe each of these four features in more detail later on.

If it is to remain wholesome or "integral," religion is, all at once, sacramental, mystical, silent and active. Each of these qualities suggests a distinct "way" of being religious,

"WAY"

but religion is most healthy and alive when it blends all four ways harmoniously. And it begins to dissolve into something other than "religion" whenever any of the four aspects is isolated from contact with its three partners. In the actual world of religious life, such sundering of one aspect from the others is not unusual. But when this splintering occurs, religion rapidly decays into magic, escapism or obsession with esoteric teachings, or into cynicism, iconoclasm or vacuous activism.

By understanding religion in this fourfold fashion we shall be able to investigate more specifically than heretofore under which conditions it may be for, against or indifferent to ecological matters. We have already seen that some contemporary scholars have argued that the present environmental crisis actually has its origins in religion. I shall argue here, though, that it is more appropriate to say that the crisis originates not in religion but in the *disintegration* of religion. And I would propose that religion begins to decompose, and thereby lose its substance, depth and intensity, whenever any one of the four elements that I have just specified forfeits its affiliation with the other three. The history of religion shows us that when any of the four constituents drops out of the picture, or when any one of them is exaggerated at the expense of the other three, then religion becomes unhealthy to the point of collapse. It is then, I am convinced, that "religion" also grows indifferent to the welfare of the natural order. Wherever and whenever religion concretely preserves the four components in a balanced way it will function in an ecologically supportive way.

I shall now proceed to establish this thesis in more detail by examining each of the four strands and its relation to the other three.

Sacramentalism

Religion is sacramental in the sense that it can speak of unspeakable mystery only through the use of symbols or what theology calls "sacraments." A sacrament, broadly speaking, means any object, person or event through which religious consciousness is awakened to the presence of sacred mystery. Historically, most of religion's sacraments have been closely related to nature. For example, the luminosity of bright sunshine, the freshness of wind and air, the purifying power of clean water, the fertility of soil and life—all of these natural phenomena, and many more, have been used by religions to symbolize the way in which ultimate mystery affects us. For example, the experience of wind or breath provides an analogy for the subtle way in which a transcendent reality can exercise its influence. The experience of being physically cleansed by fresh water gives religious people some sense of the purifying power of the sacred. And the seemingly miraculous springing to life of inert seeds that have perished in fertile ground provides religious believers with a metaphor by which to express their conviction that resurrection from death to new life is also a possibility. Religions could not have taken on their specific symbolic features apart from such ingredients of the natural landscape. Nature provides many of the fundamental sacraments of human religion.

It is easy to see, then, that the conservation of nature is indispensable for the survival of religion. I mean this beyond the superficial truism that if life on earth is destroyed religions will also vanish. For if the natural basis of our religious sacramentalism gets damaged or destroyed through our neglect, religion will lose the symbolic media by which it seeks to place us in touch with mystery. The very richness of religion's symbolic reference to ultimate reality depends upon our upholding the "integrity of creation." Water, earth, air and life must preserve their wholeness if they are to remain sacramentally transparent to mystery. A multicolored symbolic or sacramental vision is essential at the very base of religious awareness. Imagine, Thomas Berry says, how impoverished our religions would be if we lived on a lunar landscape. If we lose the environment, we lose God as well.[8] *– yes because we die!*

Therefore, because of its need for sacraments, religion can be said to be intrinsically, and not just incidentally, concerned with the task of maintaining the beauty and diversity of nature. Its connection to ecological concerns goes much deeper than ethics. Religion, by its very nature, and not just by historical accident, is inextricably interwoven with the health of the natural world. Therefore, at least to start with, one of the most fundamental responses religion can make to the current environmental crisis is to retrieve and support its own sacramentality. It cannot do so without simultaneously advocating the welfare and the intrinsic value of our natural environment. Unfortunately for both religion and the earth, as we shall see shortly, religion has been tempted at times to abandon sacramentalism by identifying itself in a lopsided way with one of the other three features of religion. And it is especially when religion loses touch with its sacramental origins that it begins to grow indifferent to the natural world.

There is another related way in which sacramentalism can be said to ground an adequate ecological ethic. Any satisfactory ecological ethic presupposes that nature is intrinsically, not just instrumentally, valuable. That is, nature must be seen as good or valuable in itself, and not simply taken as material to be molded into human products or technological accomplishments devised only to secure our own existence. A sacramental vision makes na-

NATURE must be seen good IN SE

Nature not God but images God—

ture, at least in a fragmentary way, transparent to divinity. In this sense it concedes to nature an inherent value without allowing it to become a substitute for God. Nature is worth saving not because it is sacred, but because it is sacramental, capable of mediating to our religious awareness the otherwise hidden mystery of the divine. Without allowing natural objects to become idols, a wholesome sacramentalism prevents nature from being turned into mere stuff for human consumption and exploitation. Therefore, I would argue that a sacramental vision of the world is indispensable for a healthy environmentalism.

Religion, however, can exaggerate its sacramental side. It may lose a sense of its association with mysticism, silence and action. When this happens the sacrament becomes an end in itself. It no longer functions as a symbolic access to a transcendent mystery. It loses its transparency to the "other dimension," gets closed in on itself and becomes an enslaving object of a shallow nature worship. An excessively one-sided sacramentalism leads us down the slippery slope to pure naturalism in which nature itself is identified with ultimate reality. As I have previously protested, however, naturalism does not penetrate deeply enough into the mystery of the world to tap the visionary energy needed to ground our ecological ethics.

Mysticism

To its own disadvantage and eventual undoing religion, taken in the generic sense in which I am treating it here, has not always fostered its essential sacramentalism. Why not? I think the answer lies partly in the fact that religion has the other three essential features (mysticism, silence and action), all of which exist in a sort of tension with sacramentalism. Ideally this tension allows for a healthy dynamism in religion. But, given the weakness and imperfection of mortals, the healthy exchange and reciprocity of the four elements can sometimes dissipate, only to be replaced by opposition and conflict. Let us look, for example, at the way in which the sacramental can become subordinate to the *mystical* side of religion.

A mystical leaning toward a transcendent unity that embraces but also extends beyond nature is an essential aspect of most of the major religions.[9] Without this mystical aspect of religion, sacramentalism would immediately collapse into idolatry or pure naturalism, the view that nature is all there is. There would be nothing beyond themselves for our sacraments to point to, and so the symbols would become closed in on themselves. To counter such suffocation, religion seeks to awaken in us, to one degree or another, a mystical sense, an intuition of the transcending breadth, depth, unity and healing power of the mystery in which nature is harbored.

However, there is always a danger that in effecting this essential widening of our world to give the human spirit more breathing room, religion may lose its anchoring in sacramentalism. Especially since around the sixth century BCE some religions have looked, much more intensely than they had ever done before, beyond the natural order, toward an ultimate, transcendent "oneness" that *Buddha* seems to relativize and diminish the value of nature. Caught up in the "otherness" of divine mystery, the mystic is at times tempted to despise the natural world and even to deny its sacramentality, that is, its capacity to embody and reveal the divine. At times mysticism has decayed into sheer escapism. Occasionally it has even gone to the extreme of hating the earth and everything natural.

I suspect that when religion has grown indifferent to environmental issues this has occurred most often at those times when its mystical side has been severed from its sacramental aspect. Both mysticism and sacramentalism are necessary, but they need to be delicately balanced. Mysticism must stay closely attuned to sacramentalism if it is to be environmentally wholesome, while sacramentalism has to be nourished by mysticism in order to avoid slipping down into the enclosed world of naturalism.

Mysticism disassociated from a vigorous sacramentalism promotes the gnostic doctrine of "cosmic homelessness." We observed in the previous chapter how a one-sidedly mystical sense of being lost in the cosmos allows us to interpret the natural world as little more than a restraint on the human spirit rather than as a nurturing home. When we can no longer experience our natural habitat as home, it is likely that we will not be eager to care for it. Mysticism can become so greedy for the "other world" at times that it splits off from its matrix in sacramentalism. I would not go so far as to say that antiecological attitudes originate in mysticism, because mysticism is potentially capable of remaining in healthy contact with nature and its sacramentality. But negative attitudes toward nature do accompany any mysticism that has lost touch with sacramentalism. It is quite evident that this has occurred often in the actual history of religion. But such occurrences illustrate our thesis that the ecological crisis originates less in religion than in its disintegration.

Silence

Religion possesses a third characteristic, closely related to mysticism but distinguishable from it. This is what has been called its "apophatic" quality. This means quite simply that religion necessarily requires an attitude of reserve or silence. When religion is healthy, it confesses that no single sacramental image can adequately represent inexhaustible mystery. Authentic religion demands that we not become too fixated on any particular symbol or sacrament of God. For Christians this would mean, for example, that Jesus is not the only symbol of God and that the male of the human species is not the exclusively normative representation of deity. All of nature is at least potentially sacramental. Because genuine religion is aware that no single sacrament or set of images is sufficient, it is at times moved toward a state of pure silence. Then all images and words are put aside as impediments, and silence is taken to be the most appropriate response to mystery.

But religion cannot remain completely and absolutely silent. A thoroughgoing iconoclasm (removal of images) would empty religion of any content whatsoever. It would then be indistinguishable from nihilism. Hence, religion must find a way of expressing its reserve without abandoning sacramental images altogether. It may meet this requirement by continually experimenting with an endless array of symbols or sacraments. Religious reserve in the face of mystery is practiced not just by literal silence but also by a willingness to allow an endless multiplicity of images to manifest ultimate reality, not clinging to any of them in a possessive way. The medieval mystic Meister Eckhart wrote: "Every creature is a word of God and a book about God." This statement implies that we must constantly keep moving from one symbolic representation to another in order to keep the religious sense alive and healthy. And Thomas Aquinas, in a remarkable passage, elaborates: "God's goodness could not be adequately represented by one creature alone. [God] produced many and diverse creatures so that, what was wanting to one in the manifestation of divine goodness, might be supplied by another."[10]

God as FATHER allows Mother –
Son   allow daughter
spirit
humility   allows all TANGIBLE creation

The modesty of integral religion, its refusal to encapsulate and control divinity, becomes most evident in its willingness to let go of any one symbol or set of symbols and move on to others, gingerly experimenting with an abundance of them. Religion seeks an endless plurality of sacramental images in order to gain a continually expanding sense of the infinite depths of the Godhead. Having a rich diversity of symbols in reserve allows us to let go of any one of them so that we may have the freedom to taste of others as well. In Christianity this sacramental scope is sanctioned by the notion of God as Trinity. At the very least what this difficult doctrine is saying is the following: once we have represented God as "Father," we have not exhausted what we mean by God, and so we also name the mystery "Son." Yet after doing this we still have not said everything that can be said, and so we speak of God as "Spirit."[11] Instead of feeling frustrated in the face of this teaching, as we often are, perhaps we might take it as an invitation to seek an unlimited assemblage of sacramental representations of God. There is no reason why our experience of mothers, sisters or spouses cannot also mediate aspects of deity that Father, Son and Spirit cannot. Moreover, it would seem that we are invited to experience other aspects of God by way of trees, flowers, rivers, oceans and the many other aspects of nature.

But a necessary condition of this promiscuous indulgence in a plurality of God-images is that there be available to us an extravagant natural variety. And the need to promote environmental integrity, and especially biodiversity, is obviously indispensable for such prodigality. If we fail to treasure the wide assortment of natural phenomena that make up our environment then our religions will also starve, shrivel and die.

In sum, even from the point of view of its inclination

toward silence, religion is essentially, not just accidentally, concerned with environmental well-being. When religions become content to utilize only a limited range of symbolic media they implicitly tolerate the homogeneity and banality of a collapsing ecology. Moreover, the apophatic perspective provides us not only with a rationale for preserving the earth's ecological diversity, since each aspect of nature gives us a unique angle on the world's grounding mystery; it also justifies our contemporary theological efforts to preserve the plurality of religions. For each of the religions, certainly no less than any other phenomena in nature, is a unique way toward mystery. An ecological theology must also be, in some sense, religiously pluralist as well. If the disappearance of any living species leaves the earth that much poorer, perhaps no less can be said about the death of any of the religions of the world.

Action

Fourth and finally, if religion is to have any robust connection with human life, especially with our social life, it must also have an active component. It has to be concerned, at least in some way, with transforming the world to make it a better place in which to live. We might say that the sacramental way invites us to enjoy the natural world in a spirit of gratitude for the gift that it is. The mystical way, on the other hand, exhorts us to relativize nature, that is, to keep it in perspective. The way of silence, as exemplified by Buddhism or the Jewish Sabbath, asks us simply to let the world be itself, lest in our arrogance we end up reducing it to what corresponds only to the human will. The *active* component of religion, however, persuades us to change the world. And herein there seems to lie a problem, environmentally speaking.

Is it not in this activist impulse to change the world that the possibility of environmental abuse also begins to arise? The Catholic priest, Thomas Berry, who is one of our foremost environmental thinkers today, traces the roots of our ecological problems to prophetic religion, which, he alleges, has unleashed a millennial dream of "progress" destructive of nature. He thinks that the biblical dream of progress lies behind our policies of limitless economic growth which have proven to be ecologically disastrous. And we have already mentioned that Lynn White, Jr., in his famous essay on the "religious" origins of the environmental crisis, argued that the biblical imperative to "subdue" the earth (incidentally, a misleading translation of the text of Genesis according to contemporary biblical scholarship) contains the seeds of an attitude that would eventually legitimate our human domination and destruction of the life-systems on this planet. In the judgment of Berry and White, it is the biblical injunction to transform the world that inspires our ecological recklessness.

What are we to make of these accusations that biblical religion lies at the origins of our environmental predicament? This way of articulating the cause of the crisis seems to me to be misleading. I would not oppose the hypothesis that certain interpretations of biblical religion have legitimated attitudes destructive of nature. But I would be less inclined than Berry and White to make aspects of biblical religion the originating source of our environmental crisis. Rather, to repeat what I said earlier, the crisis originates not in religion but in the disintegration of religion. I would prefer to say that the activist impulse of biblical religion (which indeed does encourage transformation of the world) is culpable only where it has lost touch with the sacramental, mystical and silent aspects that are also essential to biblical religion. In such an event, however, it has in my definition already ceased to be religion and has begun to decay into something else. For when the active side of religion is no longer nourished by the sacramental, mystical and silent qualities it has already become a kind of secular humanism which acknowledges no transcendent limits on human action.

Once again, my point is that the isolating and exaggerating of any one of the four aspects of religion, and not just the activist strand, would lead to attitudes indifferent or hostile to nature. Likewise, then, an activism that has become isolated from sacramentalism, mysticism and silence will inevitably lead to a purely secularistic, and I would suggest short-sighted, commitment to a kind of unlimited, unsustainable "progress" which the earth and its life-systems simply cannot bear. In order to avoid running away in this direction, religious activism needs to stay closely connected to sacramentalism, mysticism and the silent patience of the apophatic way.

Summary and Conclusion

When sacramentalism loses touch with the mystical, silent and active aspects of religion it becomes idolatrous. It forgets that the symbol points beyond itself. Idolatry enshrines the particular symbol-object as though it were itself ultimate. When this happens the sacrament loses its transparency to the infinite depth or mystery to which the "mystical" aspect of religion awakens us.

On the other hand, if the corrective of mysticism is not tempered by sacramentalism, silence and action it loses its ecological value by becoming mere escapism. It forfeits its connections to the physical cosmos, and this severance results in the cosmic homelessness to which we earlier traced much of our environmental neglect. When the third essential component of religion, that of reverential silence, is isolated from the other three, it shrivels into a posture inimical both to religion and nature. Silence divorced from sacramentalism, mysticism and ethical action gets reduced to a sheer iconoclasm and is on the way toward a destructive nihilism. And finally, if the activist component of religion is divorced from sacramentalism, mysticism and the silent waiting characteristic of apophatic religion, it will likely decay into an empty and vicious dream of purely secular progress, a dream of earthly perfection that has time and again proven fatal for our environment.

For religion to maintain its essential "religiousness," according to the definition we are adopting here, it needs to preserve all four aspects. The understanding of religion that I am proposing here is obviously a normative one. I am talking here about an ideal of religious integrity. A completely pure form of religion does not exist in the concrete. In fact, any particular religious tradition falls somewhat short of this ideal, since inevitably one of the four elements is usually emphasized more than the others. For example, in preliterate religion the sacramental aspect is prevalent, in Hindu Vedanta the mystical, in Buddhism silence, and in biblical traditions transformative action for the sake of justice. I am proposing, however, that for *any* religion to function in a minimally healthy way there must be at least some degree of all four aspects. This balance is essential to prevent a one-sidedness that impels religion toward an internal disintegration.

My argument here has been that the ecological crisis originates not in religion but in the disintegration of religion, and that maintaining the integrity of religion is absolutely essential for our larger global task of preserving the integrity of nature. Any meaningful religious response to the environmental crisis, therefore, requires a maintaining of the dynamic interrelationship of all four ways of relating to mystery. And the single most important thing religion can do in response to the environmental crisis is to make sure that its mystical, silent and active tendencies always remain very close to the sacramental.

We may conclude, therefore, that the essential role religion has to play in the restoration and conservation of the earth's ecology will take the shape not only of ethical exhortations (which can equally well come from secular quarters), but primarily of the unembarrassed cultivation of its inherent sacramentalism and the genuine reverence toward nature that this implies. A vigorous sacramentalism, however, requires nourishing by mysticism, silence and action. By holding all four of its elements in balance religion can demonstrate its indispensability to the task of saving our natural environment.

4

Christianity and Ecology

Precisely why should we care about the nonhuman natural world? Most of us probably believe that it is a good thing to do, and we can even give some very convincing pragmatic answers to the question. But theology is concerned with the religious justification of any ecological concern we might have. It is the task of environmental theology to spell out, from within the context of a particular religious tradition, the *ultimate* reasons why we should care about the cosmos. In my case, the tradition is Christian, and so in this and the following chapter I would like to draw out what I think are some distinctive contributions of Christian faith to the ecological movement.

I have already suggested that the threat of global ecological collapse need not lead us to abandon our religious traditions, but that it could be a major historical stimulus to their revitalization. Yet in the case of Christianity such a suggestion may seem too optimistic. Critics of this tradition, as well as some Christian authors themselves, have complained about Christianity's complicity in the western war against nature? Hasn't Christianity been too anthropocentric, too androcentric, too otherworldly and too cavalier about the intrinsic value of nature? Hasn't its theology so overemphasized the need to repair the "fall" of humanity that it has almost completely ignored the original goodness of creation? Hasn't it heard the words of Genesis about human "dominion" over the earth as an imperative to exploit and deface it?

Whether these accusations are justified or not, it is at least certain that many Christians, perhaps even the majority of them, continue to interpret the physical universe as though it were little more than a "soul school" wherein we are challenged to develop our moral character but which itself has little intrinsic significance and no share in human destiny. In this interpretation nonhuman nature is merely a set of props for the drama of human salvation or a way-station for the human religious journey.

Because of its traditionally longing so much for another world, British philosopher John Passmore doubts that Christian theology can ever reshape itself in an ecologically helpful way without ceasing thereby to be Christian. Since Christianity actually sanctions our hostility toward nature, he argues, the only healthy alternative is a radical secularism:

> Only if men see themselves . . . for what they are, quite alone, with no one to help them except their fellow-men, products of natural processes which are wholly indifferent to their survival, will they face their ecological problems in their full implications. Not by the extension, but by the total rejection, of the concept of the sacred will they move toward that sombre realization.[1]

While Passmore's indictment of Christianity may be harsh, I think we have to admit that environmentally speaking this tradition, like many others, has been at best ambiguous.[2] While the doctrines of creation and incarnation clearly affirm the value of the cosmos, most Christian spiritualities, saints and scholars have been relatively indif-

ferent to nature. The welfare of the natural world has seldom, if ever, been a dominant concern. We can boast of St.
Francis of Assisi, or of Ignatius Loyola, who urged us to
see God in all things (and that would have to include nature as well). But we cannot forget other saints like Martin
and John of Ephesus, each at opposite ends of the Mediter-
ranean during the rise of Christianity, both of whom are
famous for their prowess in the art of deforestation.[3] And
if expressions of a deep love of nature appear in some
Christian hymnody and hagiography, there are just as
many indications of a desire to escape from nature in other
facets of the tradition.[4]

Concern for either local or global environmental welfare is not a very explicit part of the Christian tradition.
Nevertheless, I agree with Paul Santmire that there is great
promise for theological renewal in the ecologically ambiguous Christian tradition.[5] In fact a rethinking of Christianity
in terms of the environmental crisis is already under way,
and it is the cause for some optimism that this tradition
may potentially be enlivened by an ecological transformation. The new theological reflection comes in several different strains, of which I shall discuss three. I will call these
respectively the *apologetic*, the *sacramental* and the *eschatological* attempts to formulate an environmental theology.
None of these can be found in a perfectly pure form, and
aspects of all three may be found in the work of any single
author. Nevertheless, they vary considerably in theological method, and so I hope it will prove illuminating to treat
them here as distinct types.

The Apologetic Approach

The first, and the least revisionist of the three, is the
more or less apologetic enterprise of trying to show that

there is already a sufficient basis in scripture and tradition for an adequately Christian response to the environmental crisis. It is exemplified by recent statements of the pope and the American Catholic bishops,[6] as well as a number of theological articles and books published in the past decade or so.[7] According to this approach, which runs the range from biblical literalism to very sophisticated theological scholarship, we have simply ignored the wealth of ecologically relevant material in the tradition. Therefore, what we need to do now in order to have an adequate environmental theology is simply dig up the appropriate texts and allow them to illuminate the present crisis. Sometimes this apologetic method merely scours the scriptures for nuggets of naturalism in order to show that the Bible cares about the cosmos after all. At its most simplistic extreme it does little more than recite the psalms and other biblical passages that proclaim creation as God's handiwork. But at a more erudite level of interpretation it excavates the themes of incarnation and creation as theological warrants for an ecological theology. In addition it digs out environmentally sensitive, and previously overlooked passages in the early Christian and other theological writings.[8] More than anything else, though, the apologetic approach emphasizes the biblical notion that God has given humanity "dominion" and "stewardship" over creation, and that this is reason enough for us to take care of our natural environment.

This first type of ecological theology also argues that if only we practiced the timeless religious virtues we could alleviate the crisis. Since one of the main sources of our predicament is simple human greed, the solution lies in a renewed commitment to humility, to the virtue of detachment, and to the central religious posture of gratitude by which we accept the natural world as God's gift and treat it

accordingly. If we allowed our lives to be shaped by genuinely Christian virtues, our relation to nature would have
the appropriate balance, and we could avert the disaster
that looms before us.

I call this approach apologetic because it defends the
integrity of biblical religion and traditional theology without requiring their transformation. It holds, at least implicitly, that Christianity is essentially okay as it is, that environmental abuse stems only from perversions of pure faith
and not from anything intrinsic to it, and therefore that
Christianity does not need to undergo much of a change in
the face of the present emergency. Rather, we need only to
bring our environmental policies into conformity with revelation and time-tested doctrine. With respect to the present state of our environment, the fault is not with Christianity but with our failure to accept its message.

How are we to evaluate this apologetic approach
(which is probably the one most Christians, and I suspect
most Christian theologians, take today)? On the positive
side, I would say that it does develop an indispensable
component of an ecological theology: it turns our attention
to significant resources in the Christian classics that have
not been sufficiently emphasized. Its highlighting the environmental relevance of traditional teachings, forgotten
texts and religious virtues is very helpful. We need this
retrieval as we begin the work of shaping a theology appropriate to the contemporary crisis.

Moreover, a good dose of apologetics is certainly called
for today in the face of many incredibly simplistic complaints by some historians that Christianity is the sole or
major cause of the environmental crisis. A sober analysis of
the historical roots of the crisis will show that some of the
antinature attitudes associated with Christianity comprise
only one aspect of a very complex set of ingredients leading

to the present destruction of the ecosphere. An unbiased historical analysis can also demonstrate that major aspects of Christianity have firmly resisted the dominating practices that led us to the present situation. Thus, some defending of Christianity seems entirely appropriate.

However, I do not think that this apologetic type goes far enough in opening Christian faith to the radical renewal the ecological crisis seems to demand. I seriously doubt that we can adequately confront the problems facing our natural environment, theologically speaking, simply by being more emphatic about familiar moral exhortations or by endlessly exegeting scriptural passages about the goodness of nature or the importance of stewardship. Such efforts are not insignificant; indeed they are essential. But I wonder if they are fundamental enough. In the face of the chastisement Christianity has received from secular environmentalists, the apologetic quest for relevant texts, teachings and virtues does not go far enough. I doubt that even the most impressive display of biblical or patristic passages about God and nature will allay this criticism or, for that matter, turn many Christians into serious environmentalists. In order to have an adequate environmental theology Christianity, I think, will need to undergo a more radical internal change.

The Sacramental Approach

The beginnings of such a change are now taking place in what I shall call the sacramental approach to Christian ecological theology. This second type focuses less on normative religious texts or historical revelation than does the apologetic approach, and more on the allegedly sacral quality of the cosmos itself. It is more willing to acknowledge the revelatory character of nature. It comes in a variety of theological forms ranging from what has been called "natural theology," which focuses on the apparent evidence for God's existence in nature, to the cosmic spirituality of Thomas Berry[9] and Matthew Fox and their followers.[10] It is also found, in different ways and degrees, in non-Christian religions, as well as in the spirituality of eco-feminists and some so-called "deep ecologists."[11]

In its typical form this sacramental approach interprets the natural world as the primary symbolic disclosure of God. Religious texts and traditions are still important, but the cosmos itself is the primary medium through which we come to know the sacred. Today the sacramental approach usually accommodates evolutionary theory and aspects of contemporary physics. It embraces a holistic view of the earth as an organism comprised of a delicately balanced web of interdependent relationships. Rejecting mechanism, it regards the entire universe organismically, that is, as an intricate network of dynamic interconnections in which all aspects are internal to each other. Hence, it also places particular emphasis on the continuity of humans with the rest of the natural world.

Accordingly, it views our spiritual traditions not as activities that we humans "construct" on the face of the earth, but as functions that the cosmos performs through us. According to Thomas Berry, for example, the universe is the primary subject, and humanity is one of many significant developments of the universe. Cultures and religions are simply natural extensions of the cosmic process rather than unnatural creations of lonely human exiles on earth.

In the Christian context today I think this revisionist approach finds its most compelling expression in what has been called "creation-centered" theology. As the prime example of our second type it goes beyond the apologetic variety of environmental theology by arguing that our present circumstances require a whole new interpretation of what it means to be Christian. In the face of the environmental crisis it will not do simply to take more seriously our inherited texts and teachings. These are still important, but they must be carefully sifted and reinterpreted in terms of a cosmological, relational, nonhierarchical, non-patriarchal, nondualistic and more organismic understanding of the universe. We must pay more attention to the sacral quality of the universe and not place such a heavy burden on premodern religious texts to give us the foundations of our environmental ethic.

In Christian circles this creation-centered outlook accepts the doctrines of the creed but gives them a cosmological interpretation. It may be helpful to look briefly at several of the results of its recosmologizing of traditional Christian teachings.

1. As the label suggests, this new theological emphasis brings the biblical theme of *creation* to the center of theology instead of subordinating it, as it has been in the past, to the theme of redemption. Theology's focusing primarily on the redemption of a "fallen" world has distracted us from an adequate reverencing of the intrinsic goodness of nature. Moreover, our understanding of redemption has been too anthropocentric. We have been so obsessed with overcoming our human sinfulness and suffering, that we have forgotten about the travail of nature as a whole.

2. Creation-centered theology also argues that we need a correspondingly broader understanding of that from which we are said to be redeemed, namely, *sin*. It insists that sin means not just our estrangement from God or from each other, but also the present condition of severe alienation of the cosmos from ourselves. Reconciliation then implies not only the restoration of human commu-

nion but, just as fundamentally, our reintegration with the earth-community and the whole of the universe. In order to experience this reconciliation we must abandon all forms of religious dualism which have sanctioned our self-distancing from nature.

3. Creation-centered theology insists also that we need to rethink what we mean by *revelation*. Revelation is not just God's self-manifestation in history, let alone the communication of divine information in propositional form. We need to think of revelation in more cosmic terms. The universe itself is the primary revelation. In its 15 billion-year evolution the cosmos is the most fundamental mode of the unfolding of divine mystery. The mystery of God is revealed gradually in the evolution of matter, life, human culture and the religions of the world (and not just in biblical religion either). Viewed in terms of cosmic evolution our religions can no longer be explained or explained away as simple heartwarming gestures that estranged humans engage in on an alien terrain as we look toward some distant far-off eternity. Rather, religions are something that the universe does through us as it seeks to disclose its mysterious depths. The fact of there being a plurality of religions is in perfect keeping with evolution's extravagant creation of variety and difference. Hence, an ecological spirituality should be no less committed to preserving the plurality of religions in the world than it is to the salvaging of biodiversity. We should lament the loss of religious diversity since religions are also products of cosmic evolution and just as deserving of conservation as the multiple species of plants and animals.

4. Viewing things in this cosmological way, creation-centered theology appreciates both ancient and modern efforts to understand the *Christ* also as a cosmic reality, and not simply as a personal historical savior. Cosmic Christol-

ogy, already present in ancient Christian theology, needs to be recovered today in terms of an evolutionary and ecological worldview. The entire cosmos (and not just human society) is the body of Christ. A cosmic Christology then provides the deepest foundations of a distinctively Christian environmental spirituality. And in keeping with this cosmic Christology the eucharistic celebration ideally represents the healing not only of severed human relationships, but also of the entire universe.

5. The theological experiment of creation-centered theology culminates in an ecological understanding of *God*. Here the trinitarian God is the supreme exemplification of ecology, a term which refers to the study of relationships. Creation in the image of God then means that the world itself has being only to the extent that, like God, it exists in relationship. An ecological theology is congruent both with contemporary science and the classic doctrine of the Trinity, a doctrine which renounces the idea that God exists only in isolated aseity.

6. This ecological contextualization of Christian teaching leads us in the direction of a whole new *spirituality*. Creation-centered theology encourages an enjoyment of the natural world as our true home. Traditional spiritualities, often characterized by a discomfort with bodily existence, received parallel expression simultaneously in the sense of humanity's fundamental homelessness in nature. The classic texts of Christianity have unfortunately been tainted by a dualistic bias that has sanctioned our hostility toward nature and the body. For this reason a purely apologetic type of environmental theology is inadequate, for it is not sufficiently alert to such ideological flaws in the classic sources.

7. Moreover, an ecological spirituality requires its own kind of *asceticism*. This asceticism prescribes a renunciation

not of the natural world but of the Enlightenment ideal of autonomous, isolated selfhood. It subjects us to the arduous discipline of taking into full account the fact of our being inextricably tied into a wider earth-community. A full life, one in which we acknowledge our complex relation to the universe, widens our sense of responsibility toward ourselves and others. Above anything else, this means adopting a continually expanding posture of inclusiveness toward all otherness that we encounter, including the wildness of the natural world.

8. Creation-centered spirituality in turn inspires a restructuring of Christian *ethics* in terms of an environmental focus. Ethics cannot be grounded only in the classic moral traditions which usually left the welfare of the cosmos out of the field of concern. An environmental awareness gives a new slant to social ethics and life ethics. In place of (or alongside of) social justice, it advocates a more inclusive "eco-justice" according to which we cannot repair human inequities without simultaneously attending to the prospering of the larger earth-community. And being "pro-life" means going beyond the focus simply on the ethics of human reproduction. An environmentally chastened life ethic questions aspects of current moral teachings that tolerate policies which, while protective of human fertility, ignore the complex life-systems in which human fertility dwells.[12]

9. Finally, creation-centered theology advocates the reshaping of *education* from the earliest years so that it pays closer attention to the natural world. At the level of secondary and college education, including the core curriculum, this would mean making environmental education central and not just an afterthought. Our students should be required to look carefully at what both science and religion have to say about the universe, and yet remain critical of

scientism and materialism, both of which are no less ecologically disastrous ideologies than are dualistic and patriarchal forms of religion.

The most characteristic feature of this contemporary revision of theology is its focus on the sacramentality of nature. (By "sacrament," let us recall, we mean any aspect of the world through which a divine mystery becomes present to religious awareness.) Ever since the Old Stone Age aspects of nature such as clean water, fresh air, fertile soil, clear skies, bright light, thunder and rain, living trees, plants and animals, human fertility, etc., have symbolically mediated to religious people at least something of the reality of the sacred. As we saw in the previous chapter, sacramentalism recognizes the transparency of nature to the divine, and it therefore gives to the natural world a status that should evoke our reverence and protectiveness. The sacramental perspective reads in nature an importance or inherent value that a purely utilitarian or naturalist point of view cannot discern. Nature, then, is not primarily something to be used for human purposes or for technical projects. It is essentially the showing forth of an ultimate goodness and generosity.

In principle the sacramental features of Christianity (and of other religions) protect the integrity of the natural world. According to our second type of environmental theology, therefore, the nurturing of a sacramental vision is one of the most important contributions Christianity and other religions can make to the preservation of the natural world. If biodiversity eventually decays into a homogeneity similar, say, to the lunar landscape (and this is the direction in which things are now moving) we will lose the richness of our sacramental reference to God. And if we lose the environment, Thomas Berry is fond of saying, we will lose our sense of God as well.

By way of evaluation, I would say that this second type of environmental theology is another important step toward an acceptable Christian environmental theology. It goes beyond the more superficial efforts of our first type which consist primarily of an apologetic search for texts that allegedly contain a ready-made environmental theology adequate to our contemporary circumstances. Our second type seeks a radical transformation of all religious traditions, including Christianity, in the face of the present crisis. The creation-centered approach is aware that religious texts, like any other classics, can sometimes sanction policies which are socially unjust and ecologically problematic. So it allows into its interpretation of the classic sources of Christian faith a great deal of suspicion about some of the same motifs that our first approach holds to be normative.

To give one example, the ideal of human dominion or stewardship over creation, which is fundamental in our first type of environmental theology, turns out to be quite inadequate in the second. Stewardship, even when it is exegetically purged of the distortions to which the notion has been subjected, is still too managerial a concept to support the kind of ecological ethic we need today. Most ecologists would argue that the earth's life-systems were a lot better off before we humans came along to manage them. In fact, it is almost an axiom of ecology that these systems would not be in such jeopardy if the human species had never appeared in evolution at all. So, even if we nuance the notions of stewardship and dominion in the light of recent scholarship, the biblical tradition is still too anthropocentric. And since anthropocentrism is commonly acknowledged to be one of the chief causes of our environmental neglect, creation-centered theology seeks to play down those theological themes that make us too central in the scheme of things. In the shadow of the environmental crisis it seeks a more cosmic understanding of Christianity.

At the same time, this approach acknowledges that we humans still play a very important role in the total cosmic picture. Our presence enriches and adds considerable value to life on earth. However, the concept of dominion or stewardship, important as it is, fails to accentuate that we belong to the earth much more than it belongs to us, that we are more dependent on it than it is on us. If in some sense we "transcend" the universe by virtue of our freedom and consciousness, in another sense this same universe is taken up as our constant companion in our own transcendence of it. Christian theology now needs to emphasize more than ever before the inseparable and (as we shall develop in the next chapter) the everlasting connection between ourselves and the cosmos.[13]

The Eschatological Approach

As I have already hinted, I have much stronger sympathies with the second approach than with the first (although the exegetical work that accompanies the first is also quite fruitful). Any attempt to construct a Christian environmental theology today must build on the sacramental interpretation of nature. Today Christianity desperately needs to bring the cosmos back into the center of its theology, and creation-centered theology is an important contribution to this process.

However, if we are looking for Christianity's possible significance in the global project of bringing an end to the crisis that threatens all of humanity as well as life on earth, I think in all honesty we have to ask whether the Bible's most fundamental theme, that of a divine promise for future fulfillment, is of any relevance here. In other words, we need to ask whether the eschatological dimension of Christianity, its characteristic hope for future perfection founded on the ancient Hebrew experience of God's promise and fidelity, can become the backbone of an environmentally sensitive religious vision. If a return to cosmology is theologically essential today, then from the point of view of Christian faith, we need assurance that this cosmology remains adequately framed by eschatology.

During the present century, we have rediscovered the central place of eschatology in Christian faith. Hope in God's promise upon which Israel's faith was built is now also seen to be the central theme in Christian faith as well, a fact that bonds Christianity very closely to its religious parent. The faith of Jesus and his followers was steeped in expectation of the coming of the reign of God. Reality is saturated with promise, and the authentic life of faith is one of looking to the fulfillment of God's promise, based on a complete trust that God is a promise keeper. True faith scans the horizon for signs of promise's fulfillment. For this faith present reality, including the world of nature in all of its ambiguity, is pregnant with hints of future fulfillment.

Until recently this way of looking at the cosmos, namely, as the embodiment of promise, had almost completely dropped out of Christian understanding. It had been replaced by a dualism that looked vertically above to a completely different world as the place of fulfillment. The cosmos itself had no future. Only the immortal human soul could look forward to salvation, and this in some completely different domain where all connection with nature and bodiliness would be dissolved. That such an interpretation of human destiny could arise in a community of faith which from the beginning professed belief in the resurrection of the body is indeed ironic. But more than that, it is tragic. For by suppressing awareness of the bodiliness of human nature dualism was inclined also to disregard the larger matrix of our bodiliness, the entire physical universe which is inseparable from our being. By excepting nature and its future from the ambit of human hope Christianity left the cosmos suspended in a state of hopelessness. It had forgotten St. Paul's intuition that the entire universe yearns for redemption. Fortunately theology has begun to retrieve this inspired idea. Now any ecological theology worked out in a Christian context must make this motif of nature's promise the very center of its vision.

It is easy enough to argue that Christianity's sacramental quality, which it shares with many other religions, affirms the value of nature. But the Bible, because of the multiplicity of traditions it embodies, has an eschatologically nuanced view of sacramentality. It is aware, for example, that something is terribly wrong with the present world and that any sacraments based on the present state of nature inevitably participate in this imperfection. Pure sacramentalism, therefore, is not enough. Biblical faith looks less toward a God transparently revealed in present natural harmony than toward a future coming of God in the eschatological perfection of creation. It is especially this hopeful tone, and not just its sacramentalism, that can ground an ecological spirituality. As we seek a Christian theology of the environment, therefore, we need to ask how the future-oriented, promissory aspect of this tradition connects with contemporary ecological concern. Most recent attempts by Christians to build an environmental theology have made only passing reference to the eschatological vision of nature as promise.[14]

Hence, as an alternative to the apologetic and the sacramental types, I am proposing a more inclusive eschatological cosmology as the foundation of a Christian environmental theology. Here the cosmos is neither a soul-school for human existence nor a straightforward epiphany of God's presence. Rather, it is in its deepest essence a promise of future fulfillment. Nature is promise. If we are sincere in proposing a theology of the environment that still has connections with biblical religion, we need to make the topic of promise central, and not subordinate, in our reflections. In order to do this in an ecologically profitable way we must acknowledge that the cosmos itself is an installment of the future, and for that reason deserves neither neglect nor worship, but simply the kind of care proportionate to the treasuring of a promise.

A Christian environmental theology, I am maintaining, is ideally based on the promissory character of nature. But some religious thinkers will complain that the biblical theme of promise is not very helpful in theological efforts to ground ecological ethics. Following Arnold Toynbee, Thomas Berry, for example, argues that it is precisely the biblical emphasis on the future that has wreaked ecological havoc. For Berry the future orientation of the Bible has bequeathed to us the dream of progress, and it is the latter that has caused us to bleed off the earth's resources while we have uncritically pursued an elusive future state of perfection. Berry holds that biblical eschatology, with its unleashing of a dream of future perfection, is inimical to environmental concern. According to this leading creation-centered geologian, hoping in a future promise can lead us to sacrifice the present world for the sake of some far-off future fulfillment. Although he is a Catholic priest himself, Berry considerably distances himself from the prophetic tradition that many of us still consider to be the central core of biblical faith and the bedrock of Christian ethics.[15]

But would our environmental theology be consonant with biblical tradition if we left out the prophetic theme of future promise? The sacramental accent taken by Berry and many other religiously minded ecologists has the advantage of bringing the cosmos back into our theology, and this is essential today. But Berry seems to be embarrassed by eschatology. Hence, in spite of his many valuable contributions to environmental thinking, I would have to question whether his and some other versions of creation-centered theology have adequately tapped the ecological resources of biblical eschatology.

In the preceding chapter's general depiction of religion I argued that the sacramental component present in Christianity and other religions is ecologically significant. Preserving religion's sacramentality contributes to the wholeness of both nature and religion. But we cannot forget that in the Bible sacramentality is taken up into eschatology. Biblical hope diverts our religious attention away from exclusive enrapturement with any present world-harmony and from nature's alleged capacity to mediate an epiphany of the sacred through its present forms of beauty. Instead, the Bible's eschatology encourages us to look toward the future coming of God. In terms of this particular religious accent any reversion to pure sacramentalism is suspect. It has, in fact, been condemned outright by prophets and reformers as faithless idolatry.

Christianity, aided by its roots in biblical monotheism, and owing to its unique emphasis on the promise of history, may itself be partly responsible for the demotion of the sacramental attitude which some religious ecologists now wish to make paramount. By understanding the promising God of history to be alone holy, Judaism and Christianity (as well as Islam) seem to have divested any present state of nature of its supposedly sacral character.

Belief in God's radical transcendence of nature, and the location of absolute reality in the realm of the historical or eschatological future—these seem to have relativized present cosmic realities, at times to the point of insignificance. The biblical desacralization of nature may even have helped open up the natural world to human domination and exploitation. Biblical religion expels the gods from the forests and streams once and for all, and because of its "disenchantment" of nature, along with its focus on the historical future, it is problematic to some religious ecologists of a more sacramental or cosmological persuasion.

Adding to this environmentally controversial character of biblical religion is the fact that, in terms of the fourfold typology of religion presented in the previous chapter, prophetic faith falls predominantly in the active or transformative type. The Bible not only gives thanks for present creation, but it also seeks to change it. It celebrates the Sabbath on one day, but it permits work on the other six. Because it is based fundamentally on the sense of promise it can never remain totally satisfied with present reality, including any present harmoniously balanced state of nature. This is because it looks toward the future perfection of creation. That is, it moves beyond any merely vertical sacramentalism that seeks to make the divine fully transparent in presently available nature. It acknowledges the imperfection of the present state of creation and seeks to reshape the world, including the natural world, so that it will come into conformity with what it takes to be God's vision of the future. Some writers have sensed herein an ecologically dangerous feature of Christianity. The Bible's prophetic tradition is then itself blamed for unleashing the dream of a transforming "progress" that has ended up wrecking the earth rather than perfecting it.

This is a serious charge, and I simply cannot respond

to it adequately here. I might just point out that apologists of our first type rightly indicate that though the biblical texts emphasize God's transcendence of nature they do not sanction the kind of exploitation of nature that some historians have traced to this doctrine. Even so, it seems appropriate for us to ask whether a pure sacramentalism would itself guarantee that we will save the environment. And, on the other hand, is it self-evident that actively transforming nature will lead inevitably to its degradation? John Passmore, whom I quoted earlier, says that

> . . . the West needs more fully to . . . "glorify" nature. But it cannot now turn back [to a sacralization of nature]. . . ; only by transforming nature can it continue to survive. There is no good ground, either, for objecting to transformation as such; it can make the world more fruitful, more diversified, and more beautiful.[16]

At the same time, he goes on to say that

> . . . societies for whom nature is sacred have nonetheless destroyed their natural habitation. Man does not necessarily preserve . . . the stream he has dedicated to a god; simple ignorance . . . can be as damaging as technical know-how.[17]

Thus an immoderate sacramentalism may be not only religiously but also environmentally irresponsible. If carried to an extreme, Passmore insists, the sacramental view can even precipitate environmental neglect. It may do so by causing us naively to trust that nature can always take care of itself. And he argues that one of the main causes of ecological destruction is the human ignorance which only a heavy dose of scientific learning can help to dispel.[18]

While many ecologists will certainly take issue with

Passmore on this matter, he helpfully forces us to ask whether we need to think of nature itself as sacred, as many religious environmentalists are now suggesting, in order to ground its intrinsic value. Can the sacramental vision proposed by Berry and creation-centered theology all by itself motivate us religiously to take care of our planet?

My own suggestion is that, without denying the ecological importance of the sacramental approach, we may follow the Bible's lead by holding close to the theme of promise. For to suppress the theme of hope and promise whenever we do any kind of theologizing from a Christian point of view, no matter what the occasion or the issue, is to fail to engage the heart and soul of this tradition. I am more sympathetic, therefore, with the theological program of Jürgen Moltmann who for almost three decades now has consistently argued that all Christian theology must be eschatology.[19] Theology must be saturated with hope for the future. And what this means for our purposes here is that environmental theology must also be future oriented, no matter how tendentious this may initially appear from the point of view of a pure sacramentalism.

I am afraid that the creation-centered approach, valuable as it is in retrieving the cosmos that has been tragically lost to our theology, has not paid sufficient attention to the radically eschatological, promise-laden, character of Christian faith. It has helpfully promulgated what has been called a "lateral transcendence," that is, a reaching out beyond the narrow boundaries of our isolated selfhood in order to acknowledge the ever-expanding field of present relationships that comprise the wider universe.[20] But this horizontal transcendence must be complemented by a looking-forward-beyond-the-present. Transcendence, understood biblically, means not only a movement beyond narrowness toward a wider inclusiveness, but also a reaching toward the region of what Ernst Bloch calls "not-yet-being," toward the novelty and surprise of an uncontrollable future.[21]

Consequently, I would like to persist in my suggestion that the distinctive contribution Christian theology has to offer to ecology (since many of its sacramental aspects are present in other traditions) is a vision of nature as promise. A biblical perspective invites us to root ecology in eschatology. It reads in cosmic and sacramental reality an intense straining toward the future. It obliges us to keep the cosmos in the foreground of our theology without removing the restlessness forced on the present by a sense of the yet-to-come.

The Bible, in fact, includes not only human history but also the entire cosmos in its vision of promise. The universe, as St. Paul insinuates, is not a mere point of departure, a *terminus a quo*, which we leave behind once we embark on the journey of hope. Modern science has also demonstrated that our roots still extend deep down into the earth and fifteen billion years back in time to the big bang. Hence, our own hoping carries with it the whole universe's yearning for its future.

The natural world is much more than a launching pad that the human spirit abandons as it soars off toward some incorporeal absolute. Through the sacramental emphasis of creation-centered spirituality (as well as the powerful voices of deep ecology, ecofeminism and the many varieties of contemporary naturalism) the cosmos now claims once again that it, too, shares in our hope. Billions of years before our own appearance in evolution it was already seeded with promise. Our own religious longing for future fulfillment, therefore, is not a violation but a blossoming of this promise.

Human hoping is not simply our own constructs of imaginary ideals projected onto an indifferent universe, as much modern and postmodern thought maintains. Rather, it is the faithful carrying on of the universe's perennial orientation toward an unknown future. By looking hopefully toward this future we are not being unfaithful to the cosmos, but instead we are allowing ourselves to be carried along by impulses that have always energized it. If we truly want to recosmologize Christianity then we do well also to "eschatologize" our cosmology. Eschatology invites us to make more explicit nature's own refusal to acquiesce in trivial forms of harmony. It persuades us to understand the universe as an adventurous journey toward the complexity and beauty of a future perfection.

Implications for Environmental Ethics

In the light of an eschatological cosmology let us then ask once again: why should we be concerned about our natural environment? Not only because it is sacramentally transparent to the sacred, but even more fundamentally because it is the incarnation of a promise yet to be fulfilled. It is because nature is not only sacrament but also promise that we are obliged to revere it. In the sacramental view we condemn environmental abuse because it is a sacrilege. But in the eschatological perspective the sin of environmental abuse is one of despair. To destroy nature is to turn away from a promise. What makes nature deserve our care is not that it is divine but that it is pregnant with a mysterious future. When looked at eschatologically its value consists not so much of its sacramentally mediating a divine "presence," as of its nurturing a promise of future perfection.

Nature is not yet complete, nor yet fully revelatory of God. Like any promise it lacks the perfection of fulfillment. To demand that it provide fulfillment now is a mark of an impatience hostile to hope. Nature is wonderful, but it is also incomplete. We know from experience that it can also be indifferent and ugly at times. A purely sacramental or creation-centered theology of nature cannot easily accommodate the shadow side of nature. By focusing on ecological harmony it expects us to see every present state of nature as an epiphany of God. This is a projection which neither our religion nor the natural world can bear.

An eschatological view of nature, on the other hand, allows ambiguity in as a partner to promise. Nature's harshness, which so offends both religious romantics and cosmic pessimists, is entirely in keeping with its being the embodiment of promise. The perspective of hope allows us to be realistic about what nature is. We do not have to cover up its cruelty. We can accept the fact that the cosmos is not a paradise but only the promise thereof.

The world, including that of nonhuman nature, has not yet arrived at the final peace of God's kingdom, and so it does not merit our worship. It does deserve our valuation, but not our prostration. If we adopt too naive a notion of nature's significance we will inevitably end up being disappointed by it. If we invest in it an undue devotion we will eventually turn against it, as against all idols, for disappointing us—as it inevitably will. For that reason an exclusively sacramental interpretation of nature is theologically inadequate, and it can even prepare the way for our violating the earth. I think that a biblical vision invites us to temper our devotion with a patient acceptance of nature's unfinished status. Understanding the cosmos as a promise invites us to cherish it without denying its ambiguity.

Summary and Conclusion

The Christian story of hope embraces the entirety of cosmic occurrence as part of its promise. Looking toward the future in hope requires that we preserve nature for the promise it carries. A religion of hope allows us to accept nature as imperfect precisely because it is promise. A sacramental theology is all by itself unable to accommodate the fact of nature's fragility. To accept nature's intrinsic value we can learn from primal sacramental traditions much that we had forgotten. But in order to accommodate both its ambiguity and its promise we are usefully instructed not only by the spirituality of primal traditions, but also by the story of Abraham.

5

Ecology and Human Destiny

In the previous chapter I argued that a Christian eco-logical theology must be rooted in eschatology. Some theo-logians, however, have seen little ecological relevance in the biblical hope for a final redemption. They think that eschatology's emphasis on the future distracts us from the urgent task of alleviating the present crisis. Eschatology causes us, they say, to postpone efforts to relieve our envi-ronmental problems.

In opposition to this point of view I am arguing in-stead that since eschatology is at the very heart of Chris-tian faith, and not something tangential or incidental to it, we will not have an ecological theology that is appropri-ately called Christian until we root it also in the sense of promise that goes back to the faith of Israel and the New Testament. It is ultimately hope in the promise of a future fulfillment for the entire cosmic story that can lead us to take suitable actions in the present to save the environ-ment. The absence of such hope will only add silent sup-port to our ecological indifference and abuse.

Since the whole cosmic story, and not just the history of humanity, can be taken up into the biblical scheme of hope, an eschatological anticipation of the coming to fulfillment of the entire universe can move us spiritually toward a suitable relation to the natural world here and now. From the point of view of Christian faith the promise residing in the present state of nature is what obliges us to treasure it. Hope in the promise of God is at the basis of all Christian theology and ethics, and hope can rightly be called the fundamental ecological virtue as well.[1] Christian faith is epitomized in the eucharistic prayer: "We hope to enjoy forever the vision of your glory." And the present beauty of the natural world provides us with an irreplaceable intimation of the vision promised to us. The natural world, in its lavish and gratuitous profusion of diversity, is an installment of the extravagant future fulfillment toward which faith perceives the cosmic story to be summoned by God.

If we view nature as promise, we are free from the obligation to worship any particular aspect of it as though it were a sacred object worthy of our adoration. Instead, we are bid to extend toward nature the same kind of reverence and care with which we would nurse any momentous promise. The drama and beauty of nature are occasions for present enjoyment. But they are enjoyable not only because we may behold in them a present beauty, but also because through them we gain a glimpse of the perfection of a beauty still to manifest itself. If we interfere with the full blossoming of nature we thereby strangle what is still promised to us in nature's evolutionary abundance and variety by the graciousness of an extravagantly giving God. We may still accept the sacramentalism which is an essential ingredient of authentic religion, but we interpret nature's beauty as the sacrament of a glory that is not yet fully revealed, and which is still hidden in the future.

Nature's Transience

If we could more deeply appropriate this eschatological interpretation of the cosmos we would be better poised than otherwise to accept nature's transience. All aspects of the natural world are finite. They, like we, are subject to the passage of time and eventually to death. Nothing in the world lasts forever. Within a finite number of years (six or so billion) the sun will become a red giant star, our oceans will evaporate, life on earth will disappear, and our planet will be melted away. Even the totality of the cosmos, in all its temporal and spatial magnitude, appears to be headed toward a death analogous to our own. The insight that made Heraclitus weep centuries ago is still valid: nothing lasts.

When we stare this fact squarely in the face we might begin to wonder why we humans, in the short span of our own lifetime, should bother to preserve and care for our natural environment. Why take action to prolong our earth's ecosystems far into the future if nature itself is so relentless in pushing all things into the pit of nothingness and death? Is it really "natural" for us humans to care so much for nature, to undertake the cause of conservation, if the cosmos itself is so intent on its own annihilation? Are we doing anything more than stemming an ineluctable tide, and is there any virtue in building our paltry dams against the flow of entropy?

A hope-filled faith leads us to affirm that in terms of the final destiny of the cosmos our present lives and actions are not at all insignificant. And what we do in the way of ecological activity, no matter how small, will be forever stamped on the course of cosmic events, even though this cosmos may be headed toward the heat death depicted by the laws of thermodynamics. The eschatological future toward which the cosmos moves is not some far-off dream waiting to happen in a fashion completely unconnected to the present. It is a blossoming of the present that will include the present, and all present moments, within itself. Hence our present environmental care is of a piece with that which we wait for in joyful hope. The continual entrance of the world's future fulfillment into the present makes the present give way and pushes it into the past. But as we shall see later, this past does not simply disappear into nothingness. Instead, it remains a factor in the final future that we anticipate. Thus the gravity of our present ecological endeavors is not eroded, but enhanced, by the fact of time's passing.

Looked at through the eyes of an eschatological faith, the passage of time actually adds value to the universe instead of signaling an irretrievable loss that might lead us to despair. The transitoriness of time that gives rise to cosmic pessimism in some quarters, may be interpreted as the condition of hope in another. For if, as faith affirms, there is an everlasting reality that "remembers" all, and thereby saves events from absolute perishing as they are pushed into the past, then the course of time adds richness to the totality of things that we call the universe. Time and perishing allow that more than one single event, or set of events, will take place. In a processive world time's duration enhances the world's worth. A cosmos reduced simply to the present moment would not be expansive enough to contain the depth and breadth that a temporal succession of happenings provides. If there were no perishing or loss, there would be no "room," so to speak, for new things to happen. There could be no increment of cosmic beauty.

Temporality allows the world to take on continually richer value. Of course, time also brings loss, but transience is part of the very definition of promise. It is an essential characteristic of any promise that it eventually dissolve in the glow of its fulfillment. Thus the unrelenting cosmic loss that causes poets to mourn and philosophers to weep is consonant with an eschatological interpretation. Some temporal passing away has to happen if a promise is to come to fulfillment.

Outside of an eschatological vision, what are the alternative ways of grounding an ecological ethic, given the transience of nature? In a purely naturalist universe headed inevitably toward the deadness of an entropic expiration, it is unlikely that we would come up with any better moral justification for conservation than the fact that we need to save life on earth simply for the sake of prolonging our own history. And if our sentiments are those of cosmic pessimism we might add that we should treasure life on earth primarily for its being a priceless exception to the general downward sweep of physical reality toward the cosmic heat death portended by the second law of thermodynamics.

The theme of nature as promise, however, allows us to take the same scientific information that feeds naturalism and cosmic pessimism and give it another reading. An eschatological faith is obliged to look into history and nature for signs that the universe, though it is dying even as it blossoms, is fundamentally a word of promise, and that in spite of entropy it moves toward a fulfillment, not just an ending. Such a reading is no more of an irrational leap in the dark than is the pessimistic interpretation given by scientific skepticism. In fact, it is completely consonant with recent developments in science. Moreover, it has the advantage of allowing us to value nature for what it is in itself rather than looking upon it only in terms of its usefulness to the survival of the human species. Let us now look more carefully at this eschatological perspective.

Nature as Promise

To have "faith," at least in the biblical sense of the term, is to become skilled in the habit of looking for promise at the heart of all realities and events, even when they are apparently dead ends. This attitude, passed on through creed, worship and the example of others, and brought to expression in the best of our theologies, goes back to the trust attributed to Abraham and his followers, to Moses and the prophets, to Jesus and to his friends who, in spite of his execution by crucifixion, were brought to new hope at the very moment when all was lost. From the ashes of their despair the latter were able to rise to the new life granted them from across the deep divide that we know as death. Out of their experience of a crucified Christ bloomed a seemingly impossible faith in the future. By way of word, sacrament and the example of others, this same faith has been communicated to others down through the ages. The central feature of this faith remains the same as that attributed to Abraham: trust that God's promises will be fulfilled. It is expressed, for example, in Luke's account of Elizabeth's words to Mary: "Happy is she who believed that the Lord's promise to her would be fulfilled." The depth of faith is measured by the degree to which one is willing to let go of the present and trust in the future fulfillment of the promise.

Thus, biblical religion deems it a virtue to look into all events for signals of God's promise and fidelity. It braces us to search for these in nature no less than in human history. If our awareness were oriented by faith, it is not impossible that we would begin to see things in the cosmos that a posture of indifference, distrust or despair would obscure. If there were any hints of a momentous future inherent in nature, and if we lacked the trust to look for them, they might never show up in our awareness. Biblical faith seeks to develop in us a capacity to see promise even in the most unpromising of circumstances. This faith is not an impediment to knowledge but a condition thereof.

If we do not risk hoping in a cosmic future, we might miss out on much that is right in front of our eyes. And if through hope we do perceive a promise inherent in nature we will be all the more motivated to care for it so that it may come to its proper fulfillment. If we sense that the universe is somehow bent on having a future in spite of the doom anticipated by the laws of thermodynamics, we will be more inclined to take care of it.

Today, as it happens, science itself is giving us a picture of a possibly promise-laden cosmos. I will grant that a consciousness unseasoned by a sense of dwelling within the context of hope for the future may give the cosmos a different reading. But there is no reason to assume a priori that a posture of pessimism, cynicism or simple neutrality will give us a more objective reading of the data than will a hope-filled venture of discovery. Indeed, if there happen to be solid reasons in the universe for us to look toward a cosmic fulfillment in the future, as I think there are, a consciousness conditioned by hope will be more likely to pick up these signals than would one shaped by indifference. One way or the other, we have to take some kind of risk of "faith" when we launch our journey toward truth. I am proposing here, at least as an experiment, that we scan the cosmic horizon armed with the hope of finding something there that is both surprising and fulfilling.

If we do so we will learn right away that the new scientific cosmography actually appears much less congenial to a pessimistic interpretation than does the conventionally accepted picture of the universe construed on the basis of mechanistic and materialist principles. Even though scientific skepticism still tries to force new information into mechanistic molds, such a constriction increasingly resembles efforts by sixteenth-century astronomers to interpret the retrograde movements of planets in terms of epicycles. The new data will no longer fit comfortably into previous expectations of black cosmic doom. Science is now finding out things about the universe that completely surprise our paradigms and invite the stretching of our cosmologies into entirely new shapes. What is most surprising is that science itself, which many pessimists used to take as a sobering road to despair, should now be raising signposts that point us back toward hope.

There are any number of specific scientific developments, especially in physics and astrophysics, that tempt us to frame the universe in terms of promise rather than pessimism. But instead of going into great detail here, we might consider just the following two global features:

1. A new openness to *mystery*. The universe no longer seems as closed in on itself as previous science had made it. We are now abandoning the belief that science can in principle explain everything. The resignation that accompanied a conviction that no mystery will be left to plumb and probe when science gets finished with its work is now giving way to a new excitement that there will always be more of the unknown yet to explore. Although a few prominent scientists still think that science will eventually eliminate our sense of mystery, others vehemently disagree.[2] Each new scientific breakthrough leads us still deeper into unfamiliar territory. Science is opening up the deep horizon of an elusive future, giving us new breathing room.

The sheer mysteriousness of the universe, of course, need not be immediately interpreted as equivalent to promise. To some it may seem a horrible abyss. However, according to the testimony of our best scientists, most of those who have come up against mystery in their scientific work have found themselves refreshed, even exhilarated by it.[3] To encounter mystery in nature is to realize that the voyage of human discovery has a future. And nothing is more important to us than to know that we have an inexhaustible future ahead of us. If there is promise in nature, then the fathomless frontier of mystery exposed by contemporary science is one of its harbingers.

2. The sense that the cosmos is a continuing *story*. If the universe were eternal, having no beginning and no ending, it would be difficult to see it as a story of promise. We might still envisage the human story (history) as unfolding within it, even meaningfully. But the cosmos itself would then be nothing but the stage on which the human story unfolds. However, it is increasingly evident that our cosmos had a beginning, even if we are uncertain about its ending. We now know that the galaxies are moving outward in space at a rate of speed directly proportionate to their distances from one another. This means that the universe is expanding. So if we could move back in time along the lines of this expansion we would arrive at a single point about fifteen billion years ago when the expansion began. This singular beginning is the so-called "big bang." It is at this unique point that the universe began its immense journey through time.[4]

Since it has this clear beginning, science is inclined more than ever before to view the cosmos as a grand story. In the nineteenth century, geology and Darwin's theory of evolution gave us reason to believe that at least the earth had a long history and that life on this planet was itself the unfolding of a fascinating story. But now, as a result of developments in physics and astronomy, we discern the inherently narrative character of all physical reality. Scientists, in spite of much initial resistance to their new task, have now become story-tellers. The cosmos they describe is no longer just a set of laws, but a narrative the quest for whose outcome is perhaps the major intellectual and spiritual inquiry of our time.

As we behold the scientists' accounts, we cannot suppress the question that readers of any great story would ask. Toward what climax is the cosmic story catapulting? What is the ending going to be like? Getting caught up in the story, we look for hints of a conclusion. If we live by hope we understandably scrutinize the past and present universe for clues about the outcome.

What do we find? At the very least we observe that over the long expanse of ages there has been a vague sort of "directionality" to the story. There have been long periods of silent waiting in which not much seems to have happened, as well as much seemingly meaningless meandering. But it is undeniable that matter has gradually become alive, and within the last 200,000 years it has even begun to think and pray. Something momentous has taken place during the fifteen billion years that have preceded us. As Teilhard de Chardin and many others have observed, the cosmic story has moved in the direction of increasing consciousness. At the same time there seems to be present in the cosmos a persistent aim toward the intensification of beauty, a movement that Whitehead has called "adventure."

Faith in the future can only interpret this adventure toward heightened consciousness and beauty as an enormous promise. The more we peer into the past that has led up to the present cosmic complexity, the more we find our gaze turning toward the future. It is the nature of the narrative to turn us from the tale itself toward questions regarding its import. What is it all about? What does it promise?

With the help of astrophysics we now suspect that even the earliest configuration of matter at the time of the big bang was full of the promise of life and consciousness. The initial conditions and fundamental physical constants that became fixed during the earliest cosmic moments were remarkably suited to the eventual emergence of life. There is no physical necessity that this would be the case, but the conditions and constants happen (for some reason?) to have fallen within the extremely narrow range of numerical possibilities that could lead to the evolution of life and finally to our own existence. And even though science itself cannot say that the eventual appearance of living and thinking beings was the "cause" that shaped the original physical conditions, it is not surprising that faith-led awareness would discern even in the initial twinklings of the cosmic story a great promise for the world's future.[5]

Biblical religion not only encourages us to look for signs of promise, but also to be open to surprise when fulfillment does occur. The life of faith does not demand that our every desire be fulfilled. Instead, it disciplines us to expect that the outcome of our hoping will always surpass our anticipations. If there is any constant theme in the Bible, it is that God's fulfillment of the promise will always go extravagantly beyond our petty sketches of the future. Thus, it is never possible for us to augur exactly what the future will be. Because the future is ultimately a mystery hidden in God, we cannot surmise with accuracy precisely what is promised. Hope is less a matter of predicting than simply of waiting (sometimes for frustratingly long periods of time) for something surprising to happen. The newly discovered cosmic story, with its vast epochs of redundancy and mere repetition, teaches us that we must be prepared at times to wait with great patience for events to ripen to the point where something new appears on the scene.

I think most scientists will today agree that if we had been present at the time of the big bang we could never have predicted, even in principle, the evolutionary outcome of the conditions we observed there. Science no longer accepts the simple notion that the final outcome of a physical process is mathematically predictable on the basis of a clear understanding of each step that leads up to it. Nature, we are now learning, does not work in that linear a fashion. Most of the things that happen, from thunderstorms to amoebas, dinosaurs and humans originate in a more spontaneous, "chaotic," nonlinear fashion out of self-organizing processes insusceptible to exhaustively predictive mathematical assaying. Most phenomena that have come forth in cosmic evolution could never have been foretold through an analysis of antecedent processes and coefficients. They have arrived quite by surprise.

My point, then, is that if an inherent incalculability has preceded all previous major developments in the cosmic story, it would do so no less in the case of any promise the natural world may hold at this present moment. What this means in terms of grounding our ecological concern is that we are obliged to provide every possible opportunity for nature to move toward yet other surprising outcomes, whatever they might be. By killing off the ecological richness of nature, which it has taken so many millions of years to attain, we prohibit fresh creation, and in doing so we violate the mysterious future which faith knows by the name God. In this sense then we may think of ecological ethics as flowing quite consistently out of the basic eschatological posture of Christian faith, its openness to surprise. We save nature because of the incalculable promise it holds.

Hope for the Cosmos

We are not thinking of promise here in the sense of an other-worldly inheritance for human souls that bears no relationship to the present state of things. We are not looking toward a spiritual heaven completely unconnected to the earth and its history. Rather, we are taking promise as the culmination of the whole cosmic story, and not just of human history. If we look at God's promise in this way, we may begin to suspect that all the transient beauty we behold in nature now, even though it may vanish from our human vision, is never completely lost, but is taken up into God's own life. What we refer to as God's "glory" is constellated in part by God's everlasting preservation of the transient beauty that makes up every phase of the long cosmic story.

If the idea of God means anything at all to people of faith, it means that loss, perishing and death are not the last word about reality. The idea of God is such a powerful one partly because it promises deliverance from absolute perishing. But while Christians have embraced this belief in the case of the survival of the human soul, they have not often been generous enough to extend to the rest of nature their trust in the nonfinality of temporal loss. An ecological perspective, on the other hand, invites us to do so. Ecology requires that we take into account the fact that all entities in nature are comprised of intricate relationships with one another. It demands that we move beyond "substantialist" thinking and see everything as connected in complex ways to the totality of the cosmos. This means that we can no longer separate human destiny from that of the entire universe.

Before ecology changed our perspective on things, we thought (along with Aristotle and Aquinas) that the world was made up of clearly delineated "substances." And we understood a "substance" as something that exists in and of itself, independently of any relations with others. At the same time we viewed the relationship of one substance to another as a purely accidental circumstance, having only a minimal effect on the definition of beings. Now all this has changed. Relationship, to speak somewhat paradoxically, turns out to be the very substance of things. Every entity is in some sense a synthesis of all the relationships presented to it by its environment. There are no substances existing independently of relationships. Christian faith, especially through its doctrine of the Trinity, implies that this is true of God also.

Developments in science, especially evolutionary theory and modern physics, but increasingly other areas as well, have allowed us to view the universe in an increasingly more relational, organismic or ecological way. For example, the basic units of the physical universe can no longer be adequately understood as tiny independently existing bits of matter colliding with or attracting one another, as atomistic materialism maintained. Rather, the fundamental constituents of nature are mutually related energy events in each of which the whole universe is somehow ingredient. Time and space are interwoven in such a way that if time stopped matter would cease to exist. "Matter" is really a *process* comprised of self-organizing patterns of relationship. It is no longer conceivable as a collection of clearly demarcated physical units having only external spatial contact with each other.

The universe now presents itself to science more as a dramatically evolving organism than as a machine. In an organism, unlike a machine, the mutual intimacy of internal constituents is decisive. Every aspect of an organism interpenetrates and interacts with the others. When one part changes, the whole changes with it. An electron inside the brain is not the mere duplicate of an electron inside a stone. Atoms are not the same when they are unobserved as when they are observed. Context and interdependency modify everything.

Our own existence as human beings is also defined by relationships. This is obvious in the sociological, psychological and biological sense. We would not be who we are without the concrete linkages we have to other humans and other living beings. Their relating to us assists in the process of own creation. But also as part of the physical universe, in which all events and phenomena bear some relation to others, we may no longer define ourselves in a simple substantialist manner. The entire universe, the whole cosmic story, in all its depth, duration and complexity, enters into the production of each one of us. There is no completely impermeable boundary between the self and its constitutive world. Selfhood arises out of its dependency on many layers of cosmic occurrence: physical, chemical, biotic, psychic, social and spiritual.

Therefore, it is incongruous to think of our own destiny, of what we hope for, or of the promise that leads us, as though the whole universe did not somehow share in this same destiny, hope and promise. Because the cosmos is more than just accidentally connected to our existence, we need not envisage our own possible redemption from perishability as though it could occur independently of the universe that enters so intimately into our self-definition. Thus, if our own personal death does not mean the absolute extinction of our being, then neither would the transience of nature mean its passage into absolute nonbeing. Is it conceivable then that in spite of their perishing, an aspect of immortality adheres to all passing things? Is it possible that their perishing is never absolute annihilation?

Death and Immortality

What is so terrifying about death is that it is not simply loss, but that this loss seems to consist of the ending of relationship. The sting of death is relationlessness. And it is partly because of our refusal to tolerate the horror of our being completely unconnected to the dead, and the dead to us, that we humans, from paleolithic times on, have produced our many symbols of immortality. The human need for relating has extended even across the abyss of death. There are implications for ecology in this need for relationship with a world that has perished.

Ecological ethicians today agree that we need a new sense of intergenerational responsibility. If we could think and feel more deeply about our affiliation with past and future generations, both human and nonhuman, we might be more inclined to act in a responsible way to save the world for the countless generations of living beings that may come after us. We are in drastic need of a conception of the cosmos and of immortality that will help us appreciate the connection we have to the extended stream of life.

So we shall be looking here for a more ecologically congenial notion of survival of death than we find in the traditional teaching about the immortality of the human soul. Religious belief in the immortality of the soul, though quite capable of sustaining a sense of the connection of living to dead humans beings, ignores the rest of creation as if it had no portion of our fate.[6] The idea of the survival of immortal human souls in a heaven completely separate from earth and its evolution does not provide the best incentive to care for our natural environment.

Nevertheless, in my opinion, much of our current indifference to the cause of conservation stems not so much from religious other-worldliness as from the radically secularistic assumption that there is an unbridgeable gap between the dead and ourselves. We live at a time in history when countless people experience a completely "broken connection" between themselves and the dead. Psychiatrist Robert Jay Lifton has traced a number of our psychological and social ills to the modern inability to imagine our connection with other generations.[7] If we are unable to symbolize immortality in one way or another, we lose any sense of our relatedness to the vast world that has gone before us, as well as to the generations of living beings that may follow. In breaking our connection with other generations we understandably forfeit our responsibility to them. Stranded in a meaninglessly brief life span, and severed from communion with the perished past or the promised future, we grow ethically impotent.

Among the many ills that we may trace to the "broken connection," I think, is our indifference to the welfare of nature. Ecologically speaking, when there is no intimated continuity with the elusive realms of past and future we have no really convincing reason to care for the universe. When the dead are in no sense still with us, the obligation to sustain their aspirations or to continue their projects finds scant sustenance. Without the feeling that we are supported by the moral energy of those who have "passed away," our own ethical commitment begins to sag. We are then burdened with the task of creating a radically new ethic out of the nothingness into which the past seems to have dissolved. If we consign the dead to utter extinction, as secularism apparently requires, we have implicitly silenced their voices. We may no longer see the point of redeeming their forgotten sufferings or even following up on their ideals. What is worse, we might also abandon any thought that our own present life and actions have significant relation to the indefinite cosmic future.

Without some healing of the "broken connection" I doubt that we can have an adequate basis for an ecological ethic. Our grasping the promise of nature requires a concept of immortality that avoids the fragmenting extremes of religious other-worldliness on the one hand and the secularist notion that all perishing is absolute on the other. In other words, we require a carefully worked out cosmological framework upon which to build an ecologically relevant notion of immortality.

Such a cosmology should be completely comfortable with modern science and at the same time appreciative of the religious quest for immortality. Once again I think that process thought provides us with at least the beginnings of such a cosmology.[8] It responds to Lifton's call to mend the broken connection, and it does so in a way that connects us not only to the human dead but to all of the perished cosmic past as well. At the same time it shows us, in a way that is compatible with scientific thought, how our present actions are taken up permanently into the future.

According to this vision, all of the events that make up natural process and human history can claim an "objective immortality." It is the nature of temporal events to add up, to accumulate, in such a way that it is never possible to undo them. Nothing will ever be able to uproot such facts, for example, as that the earth existed, that dinosaurs walked upon it, that humans evolved, or that I have lived. It will *forever* be true, even after the earth and I have passed away, that the earth existed and that I lived on earth sixty-five million years or so after the extinction of Brontosaurus. These facts will everlastingly be the case. They are brief and perhaps not very significant lines in the cosmic story, but, once written, they can never be erased.

There is something about the world that mysteriously refuses to allow even the most trivial truths to vanish. The fact that I have existed, and that I have left some sort of imprint on the cosmos, will abide indefinitely. It will always be true that I was here. It is inconceivable that there would ever come a time when this fact ceases to be true. As my actions and life become part of the fixed past, they will have acquired an objective immortality.

Even if the entire cosmos passed away, would it not still be true that it did exist? Would the truth of its having existed simply dissolve, so that it would no longer be a truth? But if it were to remain a truth forever, then what would make it true, and where would this truth reside? It is partially in our attempts to get to the bottom of this mystery that we are persuaded once again to bring in the idea of eternity, the idea of God. God would be the name of that reality which everlastingly prevents truths from lapsing. It is in God's experience that the cosmic process attains its objective immortality.

In itself such an observation may not console us if we are looking only for subjective, conscious survival beyond the grave. We may need to go beyond process thought for an adequate discussion of this further possibility.[9] Here we are concerned with ecology, and it seems to me that the idea of objective immortality is not at all inconsequential as we attempt to respond to the questions we have raised in this chapter: why should we care for nature if it all perishes anyway? and what is the basis for the intergenerational responsibility required by ecological ethics today?

If all events are deposited in an unrevisable past, a past that will always remain just what it is, the notion of objective immortality may allow us to apprehend the momentous character of our present ethical decisions. If our actions leave an everlasting imprint on the cosmos, it cannot be a matter of complete indifference whether or not we strive here and now to maintain the beauty of the natural world. Any present ecological indifference (as indeed all unethical conduct) would leave the cumulative past in an unnecessarily impoverished condition as it is held in the divine memory. Conversely, our efforts to sustain the beauty of nature would stamp a more positive imprint on the enduring repository of events. As they are pushed into the past along with us, they would leave a more aesthetically enriched mark on the cosmos and on God's own experience.

The notion of objective immortality would be incoherent in the absence of a reality that experiences, preserves or saves what is always lost to the present. And so here we understand God as the eternal care that lovingly retrieves all that has perished in time. God is the name of that reality that prevents truths from perishing and events from absolute extinction. Even though all things perish, it will always be true to God that they have happened. In God's own "feeling," all the happenings in the cosmic process are ultimately set to rest. In God all the struggle, suffering and joy in our individual stories and in the more encompassing evolutionary story abide with unceasing immediacy.[10]

In Whitehead's terms, God is a "tender care that nothing be lost." The notion that God is compassionate and redemptive can mean nothing less than that God lovingly "remembers" all of the world's experiences. In a sense, what happens to the world happens also to God. Hence, as we noted in chapter 1, God may be understood as the "ultimate environment" embracing and saving the whole series of events that make up our evolving world.

Christian ethics is rooted in the imperative to imitate God: "Be compassionate as your heavenly father is compassionate." And so it is also in imitation of a saving God, one who treasures all things in the divine "memory," that we might ground our ecological ethics. The notion of a God who is preservative Care can serve as the model of our own relation to the world. We can do no less than attempt, within the limits of our own finitude, to body-forth God's own infinite care for the world.

The traditional notion that the human soul survives death by migrating to a world completely severed from the earth is incapable of motivating us to preserve our present natural habitat. The separation of earth from heaven is ecologically debilitating. The only wholesome way we can think of heaven today is in terms that include the salvaging, not the discarding, of the earth and its history. The conviction that the world attains an objective immortality by being received into God's everlasting experience has the advantage of underscoring the continuity between the present world and our own final destiny. It forbids our old habit of separating the present natural world from considerations about the final outcome of our personal lives.

If in time dinosaurs and other species become extinct, and if sooner or later the earth itself will perish, this provides no warrant for our own contemporary disregard for the planet and its biodiversity. Our own obligation, rooted in an imitation of the preservative care of God, has to be one of striving to preserve and maintain our home to the extent that we are humanly capable of doing so. When unique and unrepeatable forms of life do pass into oblivion, we may receive some consolation from the notion that they have received an objective immortality through their reception into God's experience. But our own attempts to save the complexity of life contributes a richness to God's life that cannot occur if we persist in our present trend of indifference and even hostility toward nature. We preserve nature, among other reasons, because part of its promise is to add depth and intensity to God's own experience. And in faith's imitation of a compassionate and caring God we discover the basis for a genuinely Christian conservationism.

In doing so, however, we may suspect that the notion of objective immortality, all by itself, is hardly an adequate basis for ecological concern and action. It seems to have too fatal a ring to it. It implies that the past remains fixed, incapable of being changed. This, too, might lead us to despair unless the fixed past were also in some sense itself redeemable. It is an axiom of faith, though, that renewal is always possible, no matter how defined the past may be. But how can we make sense of such a redemption?

The answer, once again, lies in the promise that comes to us from the future. The future promised to us may be thought of as a constantly changing field of possibilities which is always able to locate the fixed past within the framework of fresh patterns that give the bygone world a continually new meaning. The past itself does not need to change for this to happen. For the entire sweep of events toward the future may take the fixed past up into the framework of a more ample vision, and this will give the finished world a continually changing significance. When we contemplate the possible source of this field of novel patterning, the name of God once again suggests itself.[11] God is the creative font of ever new possibilities who places the past in continually changing perspective. God redeems the world not only by preserving it in the divine experience, but also by inserting all that has been preserved into the ever widening compass of an elusive and open future.

Ecology and Personal Immortality

If we accept the processive understanding of the universe, the notion that all events in the cosmic story attain an objective immortality implies that there is no completely broken connection between the dead and the living. It also suggests that there is a relationship between our actions in the present and any future state of the universe, no matter how temporally remote. Here there is cosmological support for the intergenerational responsibility required by ecological ethics.

But what about the notion of individual, subjective survival of death? Is it possible to understand such a prospect in a way that avoids the ecologically questionable other-worldliness associated with most traditional formulations. Even though its view of salvation includes the notion of a bodily resurrection, Christianity inherited also the Hellenistic concept of the "immortality of the soul." In this view the soul is by nature immortal, and salvation requires the separation at death of the soul from the body. As the soul migrates from the body, the implication is that it leaves behind itself the entire material world of which the body is a part.

We have already noted how inconsistent with ecological concern this dualistic understanding of immortality seems to be. It is hardly an exaggeration to say that the death of nature is the price we have paid for the life of the soul.[12] But how else except in dualistic terms could we think plausibly of surviving death as conscious persons? Do we not need a rigorous distinction between soul and body to make such a destiny intelligible? Even to this

day many, perhaps most Christians, would answer affir-
matively. Nevertheless, an increasing number of theologians are convinced that unless we find an alternative,
Christianity's teaching about individual eschatology will
continue silently to sabotage our efforts to make the faith
relevant to ecology. A dualistic anthropology (dividing
humans into soul and body) also suggests a dualistic cosmology (separating spirit from matter) in which the entire
material world eventually becomes valueless. As long as
we persist in thinking of ourselves as essentially immortal
souls inhabiting accidentally material bodies we will fail
to give nature its due. Ironically, as I shall now argue, we
will also fail to give sufficient depth to our notion of
personality.

If we are to render plausible the notion of personal
survival of death, we must first understand something of
what it means to be a person. For classical theology this
was easy. "Person" meant an independently existing conscious substance (the soul) temporarily living a free
though embodied existence in the material world, but des-
tined for an eternal home in a heaven existing apart from
earth. This doctrine has provided great comfort and hope
to millions of people. It still does.

What then would an ecologically satisfying notion of
personal immortality look like? According to the organismic perspective we have been following, all entities are
composed of dynamic relationships. This is as true of persons as it is of subatomic particles. The notion of an independently existing substance is an illusion that we have
created because we were not fully aware of the intricate
way in which all things are formed by the specific relationships they have to their surrounding world. Ecology, however, implies that to be at all is to be related. This is true
even of God, whose being, trinitarian theology tells us, is

also constituted out of relationships. It is also the case with human personality.

A person is not simply a carefully demarcated "soul" upon which the experiences of life extrinsically and accidentally accumulate. Rather, a person is a deeply centered and at the same time deeply relational "process" of becoming whose specific way of synthesizing its environment is characterized by feeling so deep that it can become not only conscious, but even self-conscious. Another mark of personality is freedom, but freedom does not mean (as it often does in non-ecological thinking) being liberated from relationships. Instead, freedom means a virtually unrestricted ability to relate to the many aspects of one's world.[13] Personality means the capacity for continually intensifying the depth and breadth of relationship to other persons, nature and God.

We may think of God as the supreme exemplification of personality and freedom because God is, first of all, the supreme instance of relatedness. Indeed, God's capacity to relate is itself relative to nothing, and in that sense God is absolute.[14] The divine "freedom" consists of God's unrestricted ability to relate to the world. God's consciousness and "omniscience" (all-knowingness) mean that God is the most immediately and intimately related reality, receiving all cosmic occurrences into the divine feeling, even to the point of giving them an objective immortality. And the "holiness" of God means, at the very least, the unsurpassed "wholeness" of God who, unlike ourselves, excludes nothing from the divine experience. God's being is that of an all-inclusive relatedness, deserving of our complete devotion.

Correspondingly, we may understand our own personality as a finite participation in the attributes of God. To be a human person means to have the capacity to relate consciously to one's environment, in a more indeterminate or "free" fashion than do animals, plants and rocks. Inanimate objects are bound by physical laws that determine them and limit the intensity of their relationship to the rest of the universe. Animals are less tightly bound to their environment than inanimate objects, but they are still governed largely by instinct. Humans, on the other hand, though constrained by biological and environmental factors, are not subject to the rigid routine of instinct. In a still somewhat limited sense human persons are "free" to create themselves by entering more and more intensely and expansively into complex relationships with other persons and with the universe.

Given this idea of personality as the capacity to relate freely and consciously to the world, then, can we still allow for personal survival of death? And can we do so in a way that is scientifically plausible and ecologically acceptable? We can, I think, if we understand the act of dying not as a person's separation from the earth and the universe, but as a unique occasion or opportunity for entering into an even deeper relationship with them.[15] There is no reason to suspect that in such a momentous event as our own death, cosmological and metaphysical principles will be suspended. If it is as persons that we die, would not any possible "personal" survival consist of a deepening rather than a breaking of our bonds with the universe? To have a "soul" means to have the capacity to synthesize our environing world within our feeling, the competence to remember and center our life experiences, the aptitude to empathize with other living beings. Can we not conceive of the "soul's" survival, not as a suspension of these qualities, but as their qualitative enhancement. In that case death would be a personal movement toward deeper participation in God's own reception of the world into the divine feeling.

Viewed in this way, death may still be interpreted as an event of liberation, misleadingly foreshadowed by the myth of the soul's departing the body. However, in our ecological perspective the liberation consists of death's setting the person free from its limited relationship with a proximate terrestrial environment in order to allow a less restricted relationship to the entire cosmos. In this ecological interpretation of death we are released from our narrow relationship to a local frame of reference and given leave to relate more intimately to the whole universe. Death, whose sting is relationlessness, becomes the momentous event of entering finally and decisively into a most intimate relationship with the world and with the God whose compassionate sensitivity always includes the world. Thus, death would be an occasion for the advancement and fulfillment, not the disintegration of personality. Though this is theologically speculative, it is at least consistent with a hope anchored in the sense that nature is promise and not simply a constraint on the human "soul."

The spiritual wisdom of saints and philosophers has advised us that the way to live our lives is to prepare for death. In a dualistic perspective, this preparation usually takes the form of detaching ourselves from the world and even from our bodies in order to be ready for the final flight of the soul out of its prison on its other-worldly journey. But in an ecological perspective the preparation for death consists of augmenting and deepening our relationships to the world during our lifetime. If death is conceivably a decisive deepening of the person's relationship with the world, then we ready ourselves for this event not by reducing the degree of our connectedness to the earth and human community, but by heightening it. We may still emphasize the need for "spiritual" detachment, just as earlier we embraced the ideal of "religious homelessness," without having this mean a weakening of our ties to nature. We do not need to forget all that our religious traditions have taught us about the need for discipline and even asceticism. But in an ecological spirituality our asceticism consists not so much of leaving things out or excluding things, as of painfully including those things that we ordinarily leave out, both cultural and natural, within the ambit of our care.

Christians will recognize the model for such an inclusive life in the gospels' portraits of Jesus. There he is pictured as one who constantly sought out deeper relationship with others, especially with those who were no longer connected to life: the social outcasts, the sick, the sinners and the dead. The central image of his life is one of including the unincluded. This life is also the model for our ecological concern. Ecological ethics in a Christian context is the extension to all beings of the inclusive life-style of Jesus. In Christian faith, Jesus' radically inclusive life is the sacrament of what God is like. There is no need to add that the authentic life, one of expanding relationships to the point of all-inclusiveness, is a dangerous one. It led Jesus to his execution.

In the light of these reflections we may speculate even further on the state of our existence "after" death. Obviously any such speculation is extrapolation, but on the basis of the view of personality we have just laid out, we may legitimately infer that postmortem existence would not be a static dead-end, as numbing pictures of the beyond have often projected. In an ecological, process-relational vision, God's own life is one of continually deepening relationship to the world. Therefore, our own relationship to our ultimate environment, to the God who includes the world-process within the divine feeling, would share in this adventure of continually assimilating the cosmic story instead of distancing ourselves from it by retiring into some totally spiritualized heaven. "Entering into our rest" need not exclude the enjoyment of continual adventure. If this is the case, then the state of our natural world cannot be an unimportant matter for those whose hope includes a personal survival of death.

Christian eschatology looks forward to a "resurrection" of the body. Once again the process-relational cosmology we have adopted and adapted may give us a fresh ecological slant on this teaching. What does it mean to have a body? Having a body is, first, a condition of being related to the world and, second, it is what allows us to live "narratively." In other words, existing in a "bodily" way means being able to have at the core of one's identity the *story* of accumulated experiences of relationship with the world. It is our bodies that allow us to relate to the world and that allow these relationships to define us. Even from the point of view of physics we may now move beyond the simplistic materialism that reduces bodiliness to an interesting collection of replaceable units of "matter." Instead, we now view our bodiliness as the human mode of something that characterizes all of the cosmos: relatedness, process and transience. Bodiliness ties us into the cosmos. It is the condition and the consequence of a complex relationship to the universe. Our bodies are the repositories of a sequence of perished events that add up to a *story* of interconnectedness with our world.

What then would it mean to say that our bodies are raised from the dead? Obviously, since surprise is an essential aspect of eschatology, we cannot and should not try to be very specific. But at the very least we can say that thinking of bodily resurrection in terms of the resuscitation of a corpse is shallow and misleading. Rather, bodily resurrection may mean the reception of our life *stories*, both individually and collectively into the everlasting sympathy and care of God's feeling. Thus, the basis for belief in bodily resurrection is the compassion of God, God's inability to forget what has happened to us and the world. The power of God to raise us from the dead is of a piece with God's loving embrace of the entire cosmic story which, in perishing, passes into the everlasting divine feeling. To be raised bodily from the dead is to experience the constantly new meaning of deeper connectedness to the total cosmos as it is received into God's love.

Summary and Conclusion

In our process-relational cosmology physical reality is made up not of chunks of matter, but of moments of experience. Since the universe is composed of happenings which keep adding up or accumulating, it attains an objective immortality in God's experience. If atoms and cells are composed of temporal events, this would be no less the case with human bodily existence. The basis of our "resurrection" would be God's own relatedness to the world, a relatedness which consists of God's compassionate saving of all events everlastingly in the divine experience. And our personal immortality could be understood as the deepening through death of our relatedness to the cosmos. This way of looking at resurrection and immortality has the advantage of enhancing the ecological sense of our connection to the cosmos and other generations of living beings. Our own personal destiny cannot be separated from that of the entire cosmic story. Thinking of our own bodily resurrection as inseparable from the fate of the entire universe might make us less indifferent toward the natural world to which we will forever be related.

Notes

Introduction

1. Russell Train, *Vital Speeches of the Day* (1990), pp. 664–65.
2. Ibid., p. 664.
3. (New York: Paulist Press, 1984).

1. Ecology and Cosmic Purpose

1. Stephen Weinberg, *The First Three Minutes* (New York: Basic Books, 1977).
2. Alan Lightman and Roberta Brawer, *Origins: The Lives and Worlds of Modern Cosmologists* (Cambridge: Harvard University Press, 1990). When asked by the authors about the "point" of the universe, astronomer Margaret Geller responds: "What point? It's just a physical system, what point is there?" There is a sense, of course, in which "pointless" can also mean incalculable or mysterious, and so in that sense the term is perhaps not so alarming. However, to say that the universe is pointless expresses, more than anything else, a kind of resignation that seems to place in question the value of nature.
3. George Gaylord Simpson, *The Meaning of Evolution*, Revised Edition (New York: Bantam Books, 1971), pp. 314–15.
4. Thomas Berry, *The Dream of the Earth* (San Francisco: Sierra Club Books, 1988).

5. Lynn White, Jr. "The Historical Roots of Our Ecological Crisis," *Science*, Vol. 155, pp. 1203–1207.

6. Berry, pp. 204–06.

7. Biologist S.E. Luria, for example, writes: "The essence of biology is evolution, and the essence of evolution is the absence of motive and purpose." *Life: The Unfinished Experiment* (New York: Charles Scribner's Sons, 1973), p. 148.

8. Stephen Jay Gould, *Ever Since Darwin* (New York: Norton, 1977), pp. 12–13.

9. E. O. Wilson, *On Human Nature* (New York: Bantam Books, 1979), p. 2.

10. I cannot discuss at this point the issues surrounding the so-called (and inappropriately named) "anthropic principle," some versions of which seem, to some, to be open to a teleological interpretation. In any case, the authors just listed have little sympathy for it, and when they do accept a weak version of it they generally see no teleological implications in it.

11. Francis Crick, *Of Molecules and Men* (Seattle: University of Washington Press, 1966), p. 10.

12. Jean-Pierre Changeux, *Neuronal Man*, trans. L. Garey (New York: Pantheon Books, 1985).

13. Methodologically it is sound procedure to go as far as we can in explaining life and mind in terms of their chemical constituency. The only caution, and it is a significant one, is that if there is more to these phenomena than chemistry by itself can explain, it is only honest to acknowledge it.

14. William James, *Pragmatism* (Cleveland: Meridian Books, 1964), p. 76

15. I have summarized Whitehead's position more fully in my book on science and religion, *The Cosmic Adventure* (New York: Paulist Press, 1984). See also Alfred North Whitehead, *Adventures of Ideas* (New York: The Free Press, 1967), pp. 252–96.

16. E. D. Klemke, "Living Without Appeal," in E. D. Klemke, ed., *The Meaning of Life* (New York: Oxford University Press, 1981), pp. 169–72.

17. Barry Commoner, "In Defense of Biology," in Ronald

Munson, ed., *Man and Nature* (New York: Dell Publishing Co., 1971), p. 44.

18. I do not subscribe, for example, to some aspects of process theologians' interpretations of divine creation, nor to Hartshorne's disregard for the religious hope for subjective immortality. What I find most appealing about process theology is its conception of nature and its vision of a God who is truly related to the world. I will discuss these latter features again in chapter 5.

19. For an introduction to process theology see John B. Cobb and David Griffin, *Process Theology: An Introductory Exposition* (Philadelphia: The Westminster Press, 1976). For the best discussion of the environmental implications of process theology see Charles Birch and John B. Cobb, Jr., *The Liberation of Life* (Cambridge: Cambridge University Press, 1981).

20. See Schubert Ogden, *The Reality of God* (San Francisco: Harper & Row, 1977), p. 47.

21. Alfred North Whitehead, *Process and Reality*, corrected edition, ed. by David Ray Griffin and Donald W. Sherburne (New York: The Free Press, 1978), p. 346.

22. Birch and Cobb, *The Liberation of Life*, p. 196.

23. For elaboration see chapter 5.

2. Cosmic Homelessness

1. Lynn White, Jr. "The Historical Roots of Our Ecological Crisis," *Science*, Vol. 155, pp. 1203–1207. See also the articles by and about Thomas Berry collected in *Cross Currents* XXXVII, Nos 2 & 3 (1988), pp. 178–239.

2. "A Free Man's Worship," in Bertrand Russell, *Why I Am Not a Christian* (New York: Simon and Schuster, 1957).

3. Albert Camus, *The Myth of Sisyphus and Other Essays*, trans. Justin O'Brien (New York: Knopf, Inc, 1955).

4. Chapters 4 and 5 will look more closely at the "promising" side of nature.

5. It might be more accurate to say, as we shall argue in the

following chapter, that the origins of the environmental crisis lie not in religion so much as in the *disintegration* of religion.

6. Michael Polanyi, *Personal Knowledge* (New York: Harper Torchbooks, 1964), p. 142.

7. See Alfred North Whitehead, *Modes of Thought* (New York: The Free Press, 1968), p. 123: "The degeneracy of mankind is distinguished from its uprise by the dominance of chill abstractions, divorced from aesthetic content."

8. Walker Percy, *Lost in the Cosmos: The Last Self-Help Book* (New York: Washington Square Press, 1984), p. 8.

9. See Rudolf Bultmann's programmatic essay, "New Testament and Mythology," in Hans Werner Bartsch, ed., *Kerygma and Myth*, trans. Reginald Fuller (New York: Harper Torchbooks, 1961), pp. 1–44.

10. See Denis Edwards' fine presentation of the ecological significance of Rahner's theology, *Jesus and the Cosmos* (New York/Mahwah: Paulist Press, 1991).

11. Karl Rahner, *Theological Investigations*, Vol. XXI, trans. Hugh M. Riley (New York: Crossroad, 1988), p. 50 (Emphasis original).

12. Ibid., (emphasis added).

13. Recently theologies influenced by some forms of "postmodern" thought such as French deconstructionism exemplify the same tendencies.

14. See Gordon Kaufmann, *An Essay on Theological Method* (Missoula, Montana: Scholars Press, 1975).

15. Gordon Kaufmann, *God the Problem* (Cambridge: Harvard University Press, 1972), p. 122.

16. A lack of cosmic awareness is present also in much liberation theology. However, as an increasing number of theologians sympathetic to this perspective are now insisting, a socioeconomic concern can no longer plausibly be separated from a cosmic concern. Today a synthesis of concern for the environment and human liberation has produced a more integral theology focused on "eco-justice."

17. Whitehead, *Process and Reality*, pp. 79–80, 196–97.

18. Alfred North Whitehead, *Adventures of Ideas* (New York: The Free Press, 1967), pp. 265, 241–72.

19. Holmes Rolston, *Science and Religion* (New York: Random House, 1987), p. 119.

20. Brian Swimme, "The Cosmic Creation Story," in David Ray Griffin, ed., *The Reenchantment of Science* (Albany: SUNY Press, 1988), pp. 47–56.

21. Ibid., p. 52.

22. Ibid., p. 50.

23. Ibid.

24. See my book, *The Cosmic Adventure* (New York: Paulist Press, 1984).

25. Whitehead, *Adventures of Ideas*, p. 258.

3. Religious and Ecological Integrity

1. See, for example, Herman E. Daly and John B. Cobb, Jr., *For the Common Good* (Boston: Beacon Press, 1989).

2. See, for example, Vice-President Albert Gore's fine book, *Earth in the Balance: Ecology and the Human Spirit* (New York: Houghton Mifflin Company, 1992.), pp. 238–55.

3. See the similar point made by John Bowker in *Is Anybody Out There?* (Westminster, Md.: Christian Classics Inc., 1988), p. 17.

4. Cited in Roderick Frazier Nash, *The Rights of Nature* (Madison: University of Wisconsin Press, 1989), p. 120.

5. Most theologians now accept the World Council of Churches' linking of justice and peace to the theme of the "integrity of creation."

6. John Hick, *An Interpretation of Religion* (New Haven: Yale University Press, 1989), pp. 36–55.

7. John Bowker, *Is Anybody Out There?*, pp. 1–80.

8. Thomas Berry, *The Dream of the Earth*, p. 11.

9. Buddhism is perhaps an exception, at least as far as many of its formal teachings are concerned. But just as popular Buddhism is filled with many sacramental aspects, it can be plausibly argued that a sense of "mystery" hovers over most of its expressions as well.

10. (*Summa Theologica I*, 48, ad 2).

11. I owe this interpretation to a public address given by theologian Michael Himes.

4. Christianity and Ecology

1. John Passmore, *Man's Responsibility for Nature* (New York: Scribner, 1974), p. 184.

2. See Paul Santmire, *The Travail of Nature* (Philadelphia, Fortress Press, 1985).

3. Robin Lane Fox, *Pagan and Christian* (San Francisco: Harper & Row, 1988), p. 44.

4. Very early in the history of Christianity there appeared the "heresies" of docetism and monophysitism, which denied the incarnation of God in Christ, and gnosticism, which advocated escape from the allegedly evil material world. In spite of their being officially condemned by the Christian church, however, docetism and monophysitism still hover over our Christology, and gnosticism continues to infect Christian spirituality. The previous failure of Christianity effectively to confront the ecological crisis is in part the result of its continuing flirtation with these excessively spiritualist perspectives, both of which are embarrassed at our historicity, our "naturality" and our embodied existence.

5. Paul Santmire, *The Travail of Nature* (Philadelphia: Fortress Press, 1985).

6. See the World Day of Peace Message by Pope John Paul II entitled *The Ecological Crisis: A Common Responsibility* (1990), and the American Catholic bishops' recent statement, *Renewing the Earth* (1992).

7. One of the best examples of the apologetic type, from a quite conservative Catholic standpoint, is Charles M. Murphy's, *At Home on Earth* (New York: Crossroad, 1989). From a more "liberal" Catholic perspective, but still within the framework of what I am calling the apologetic kind of environmental theology, is John Carmody's provocative *Religion and Ecology* (New York: Paulist Press, 1983). Most current Christian theology of the environment is apologetic in nature.

8. See, for example, Bernard J. Przewozny, "Elements of a

Catholic Doctrine of Humankind's Relation to the Environment," in B. J. Przewozny, C. Savini and O. Todisco, *Ecologia Francescana* (Rome: Edizioni Micellanea Francescana, 1987), pp. 223–255.

9. Thomas Berry, *The Dream of the Earth*.

10. Matthew Fox, *Original Blessing* (Santa Fe: Bear & Co., 1983); and Brian Swimme, *The Universe Is a Green Dragon* (Santa Fe: Bear & Co., 1984).

11. For a compendium of such viewpoints see Charlene Spretnak, *States of Grace* (San Francisco: Harper & Row, 1991).

12. Whenever it ignores the fact that overpopulation adds enormously to every kind of ecological degradation, Christian moral teaching ironically contributes to what the Irish missionary to the Philippines, Sean McDonagh, has called the "death of birth," and therefore does not deserve to be called "pro-life" in the deepest sense of the term. See his *The Greening of the Church* (Maryknoll: Orbis Books, 1990), pp. 38–73.

13. See Fritjof Capra and David Steindl-Rast, *Belonging to the Universe* (San Francisco: HarperCollins).

14. A major exception is Jürgen Moltmann, *God in Creation*, trans. Margaret Kohl (San Francisco: Harper & Row, 1985).

15. Berry, p. 204.

16. Passmore, p. 179.

17. Ibid., pp. 175–76.

18. Ibid.

19. Jürgen Moltmann, *Theology of Hope*, trans. James W. Leitch (New York: Harper & Row, 1967).

20. The concept of lateral transcendence is that of Linda Holler, cited by Spretnak, p. 155.

21. See Ernst Bloch, *The Principle of Hope*, Vol. I, trans. Neville Plaice, Stephen Plaice and Paul Knight (Oxford: Basil Blackwell, 1986).

5. Ecology and Human Destiny

1. This point is made explicitly in the recent pastoral of the American Catholic Bishops, *Renewing the Earth*.

2. Astrophysicist Stephen Hawking, who in many ways has opened our eyes to the mystery of the universe, concluded his best-selling book, *A Brief History of Time* (New York: Bantam Books, 1988), with the words: ". . . our goal is a complete *understanding* of the events around us, and of our own existence." p. 169. Physics, he avows, may eventually answer the question why the world exists, which would be the equivalent of knowing "the mind of God." (p. 175). Then, presumably, there will be no more mysteries to explore. Paul Davies, on the other hand, exemplifies those scientists who, in the spirit of Albert Einstein, take issue with the bold prediction that physics will eventually lead to the elimination of mystery. See his recent book, *The Mind of God* (New York: Simon & Schuster, 1992).

3. Albert Einstein, for example, wrote: "The most beautiful experience we can have is of the mysterious. . . . Whoever does not know it and can no longer wonder, no longer marvel, is as good as dead, and his eyes are dimmed . . . it is this knowledge and this emotion that constitute true religiosity; in this sense and in this sense alone, I am a deeply religious man." *The World as I See It* (New York: Covici Friede, 1934).

4. The "big bang" theory, which postulates a beginning to the cosmos, has apparently received dramatic new confirmation through the data coming in from the COBE satellite project.

5. I would emphasize that I am not maintaining that science itself can clearly validate this. I am not proposing that the so-called "strong" anthropic principle has scientific status. However, if the Christian doctrine of creation is a truthful interpretation of the universe, and if the existence of life and mind are the product of a divine design, it would not be surprising if the initial cosmic conditions and fundamental physical constants took on a specifically promising character that reaches at least partial fulfillment in the emergence of living and thinking beings.

6. The apocalyptic notion of resurrection, though it takes the body into the scheme of final deliverance, has often been interpreted in such a way that it seems to exaggerate the discontinu-

ity between humans and nature, and between "this present age" and the "age to come."

7. Robert Jay Lifton, *The Broken Connection* (New York: Simon & Schuster, 1979).

8. Here I am loosely adapting some ideas that I first encountered in the writings of Alfred North Whitehead and Charles Hartshorne.

9. The question of personal immortality, one to which process theology has not always done justice, will be taken up below.

10. See chapter 1. Whitehead and process theology call this aspect the "consequent nature" of God.

11. Process theology refers to this aspect as the "primordial nature" of God.

12. See Carolyn Merchant, *The Death of Nature* (San Francisco: Harper & Row, 1980).

13. Since all entities are comprised of relationships, it is possible to attribute at least some degree of "freedom" (indeterminacy might be a better term), in the sense of a capacity to enhance relationship, to every actuality. This capacity to intensify relationship would, of course, be vanishingly small in the case of inanimate reality, but it would become progressively more expansive in plants, animals and humans, and it would be absolutely unrestricted in the case of God. We might understand the story of evolution, then, as one of emergent freedom, that is, of the capacity to deepen relationship.

14. Ogden, p. 47.

15. Karl Rahner, S.J., has suggested a position similar to this process perspective, in his still somewhat dualistic sounding notion that upon death the soul takes on a "pancosmic" relationship to the world rather than becoming completely detached from the world. See *On the Theology of Death* (New York: Herder and Herder, 1961), pp. 18–19. A number of Rahner's ideas, on death and other subjects, lend themselves to development in terms of a process-relational metaphysics.

Index